An Introduction to Chess

Shaun Taulbut

THE CROWOOD PRESS

First published in 1984 by
THE CROWOOD PRESS
Crowood House,
Ramsbury, Marlborough,
Wiltshire SN8 2HE

British Library Cataloguing in Publication Data

Taulbut, Shaun
An Introduction to Chess.
1. Chess
I. Title
794.1'2   GV1449.5

ISBN 0-946284-85-7

Photoset by Andek, London

Printed in Great Britain

To Viv & Jan

Contents

Acknowledgements

I would like to thank the Publisher for suggesting the project; my brother Neil for the view of a non chess player (until now!); and my wife Christine for all her help.

1 HOW TO PLAY

Chess is a game for two opponents. It is played on a board composed of 64 squares coloured alternately black and white. The board is placed between the two players so that there is a white square in each one's right hand corner.

Now the board has been positioned correctly the chess men or pieces may be placed on the board. The two armies face each other at the beginning of the game:

Each player has an army made up of:

1 King (♔ ♚)   2 Bishops (♗ ♝)   2 Rooks (♖ ♜)
1 Queen (♕ ♛)   2 Knights (♘ ♞)   8 Pawns (♙ ♟)

In order to describe the battlefield a number of terms are useful:

FILES

The lines of squares going up and down the board are called files:

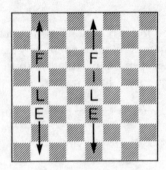

RANKS

The lines of squares going across the board are called ranks:

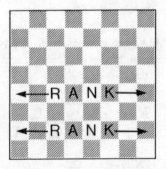

DIAGONALS

The lines of squares slanting across the board are called diagonals. A diagonal cuts through the corners of squares:

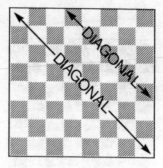

Certain ranks and diagonals have names:

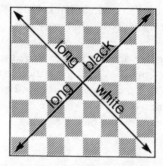

The two diagonals from corner to corner are called the *long diagonals*, or respectively the long white diagonal (from the top left to the bottom right hand corner) and the long black diagonal (from the bottom left to the top right hand corner).

The pieces are placed on the board as follows. Start with the white square on the right hand corner and place a rook on it; another rook is placed in the corner on the same rank. Next to each rook goes the knight, and next to each knight is a bishop. In the middle of the back rank are the king and queen. It is essential to remember the position of the queen. The white queen always starts on a white square at the beginning of the game (the black queen starts on a black square). The king sits next to the queen. On the second rank there is a row of eight pawns.

Start off with an empty board and set up the white pieces first. They all belong on one side of the board. Then set up the black army on the other side of the board. You should now have this position:

White always moves first, then Black, then White again, and so on until the game ends. Note that only one piece may be on a square at a time.

The object of a game of chess is to capture the enemy king. The game ends when a king is in such a position that it cannot avoid being captured. When the king cannot avoid being captured it is said to be 'checkmated'.

Now we shall see how the pieces move.

THE KING

This moves one square at a time in any direction, as in the diagram:

The king may move to any of the eight squares as indicated by the arrows.

4

The king can capture enemy pieces which are adjacent to it:

The king can capture the black bishop or the black rook. It does this by removing the enemy piece from the board and placing itself on the new square.

The king cannot move into a position where it may be captured. A piece that threatens to capture the king is said to be 'checking' the king. A king which is under threat from a piece is said to be 'in check'.

Thus, in the diagram above, the white king cannot move to the squares marked with a cross.

The king has a special move called *castling*, which we shall look at later.

THE QUEEN

The queen moves horizontally, vertically or diagonally any number of squares it wishes. Thus in the diagram below it may move to any square marked with a cross. The queen is the most powerful chess piece, and from the middle of the board is able to reach 27 squares:

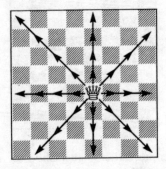

The queen can move to any of the squares marked

THE ROOK

The rook is the next most powerful piece after the queen. It can move to a maximum of 14 squares when it is standing in the middle of the board. The rook has a special move with the king, which we shall look at later, called castling.

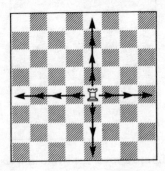

The rook can move to any of the squares marked

THE BISHOP

The bishop moves any number of squares it wishes along the diagonals. It can never change from the colour of the square on which it is initially placed. Each side has one bishop which moves on the dark squares, and one bishop which moves on the light squares:

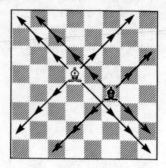

The bishops can move to any of the squares along the diagonals marked in the diagram above.

THE KNIGHT

The knight is different from all the other pieces in two respects:
a) it can jump over the other pieces;
b) it does not move in a straight line. The knight's move is L-shaped. It either goes two squares up or down the board and then one square across, or alternatively two squares across and then one square up or down:

The knight can move to any square marked with a cross. Note that if the knight is on a white square it moves to a black square; if it is on a black square, it moves to a white square. The knight can capture any enemy piece on the square where it lands.

7

CAPTURES

A chessplayer can choose whether or not to capture an enemy piece. You do not have to capture, and there is no penalty for not capturing. You capture by taking the opponent's piece off the board and moving your own man into its place:

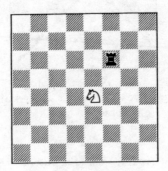

fig 1 Before Capture

fig 2 After Capture

The white knight may capture the black rook (*fig 1*). It does this by removing the enemy piece from the board and occupying the square the enemy piece was on (*fig 2*).

Here the white rook can capture the black bishop or knight.

The rook cannot jump and thus cannot go past the white pawn or the black knight or bishop, the knight being the only piece which can jump.

THE PAWN

The pawn can only move forwards. Normally a pawn's advance is limited to one square at a time, but for its first move the pawn is allowed to move either one or two squares. The pawn is the only piece whose capturing move is different from its normal move. Pawns capture enemy pieces who are one square *diagonally* ahead of them:

The white pawn may capture either the black knight or bishop, or it may move one square forward.

9

PAWN PROMOTION

A pawn which reaches its own eighth rank must be exchanged for another piece: a rook, knight, bishop or queen, but not a king:

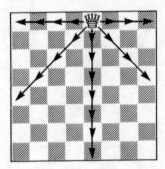

The pawn is removed from the board and the chosen piece is put in its place. The player usually decides to promote the pawn into a queen because that is the strongest piece.

On the next move the new queen can move to any of the squares marked with crosses in the diagram above. By promoting pawns it is possible to have two or more queens, or three or more knights, bishops or rooks. In theory it is possible to have 9 queens on the board at the same time (the original plus eight promoted pawns). But this is very unusual; you would need 8 extra chess sets for the new queens!

THE EN PASSANT RULE

If you have a pawn on your fifth rank when your opponent advances a pawn on an adjacent file two squares from its starting position then you can, if you wish, take off the enemy pawn as if it had only advanced one square. You have this option only on the move immediately after the pawn has advanced two squares – you cannot defer capturing it. Note that if a pawn has taken two moves instead of one to advance to the fourth rank then it cannot be captured *en passant*.

The white pawn can take the black pawn which has moved two squares on its first move. It does this by capturing diagonally one square behind the black pawn and then removing the black pawn. The completed white move is shown in the next diagram.

The *en passant* capture was introduced when the rules were changed in the sixteenth century to allow a pawn to move two squares on its first move.

11

CASTLING

Castling is a special move made by the king and the rook, before they have moved from their starting positions:

After Kingside Castling:

After Queenside Castling:

In castling, the king moves two squares in the direction of the rook. The rook then jumps over the king to the square immediately on the other side of the king. This is all one move. Castling may be done once only by either player during a game. To castle, move the king first.

There are a number of rules about castling and the situations in which you may not castle. You may not castle if:

1) There is a piece occupying a square between the king and the rook.

2) If you are in check. (If you can get out of check without moving your king, then you can castle later in the game.)

3) If your king has to cross a square which is attacked by an enemy piece.

4) If you have already moved your king or rook.

5) If the square on which the king lands is attacked by an enemy piece, i.e. the king would be in check after castling.

VALUE OF THE PIECES

The value of the pieces depends on the position but a useful guide is:

Pawn   = 1
Knight = 3
Bishop = 3
Rook   = 5
Queen   = 9

The king is not given a value because it is invaluable; if you lose your king it is the end of the game.

The value of the pieces is based on the number of squares each commands. Take an open board and place each piece in turn on its own in the middle of the board and see how many squares the piece can move to.

It can easily be seen that the queen controls almost twice as many squares as the rook and thus is worth almost twice as much.

The bishop and knight differ in the number of squares they control. Consequently a bishop is worth more in open positions, or positions where there are few pieces. The knight is much better in closed or blocked positions because of its ability to jump.

It is also worth placing the pieces on the edge of the board to see how their power declines.

A good exercise is to see for yourself how powerful the pieces are in various positions; write out a table of square control for each piece.

NOTATION: WRITING THE MOVES

In order to record a game it is necessary to give each square a reference number/letter. Every square on the board has its own unique combination of reference number and letter:

The files are lettered a-h and the ranks 1-8 so that each square has a letter and number.

If White moves his knight from g1 to f3 we write this down as ♘f3. If two white knights can move to f3 we write ♘gf3 or, if White's other knight is on the g-file (i.e. on g5), ♘1f3.

> ♘ is used for Knight
> ♗ is used for Bishop
> ♖ is used for Rook
> ♕ is used for Queen
> ♔ is used for King

If there is no prefixing symbol, then a pawn move is indicated, e.g. e4 is a pawn move to e4.

A piece being moved from one square to another constitutes one move. In writing the move, the piece symbol comes first followed by the square of departure. The square of departure is linked to the square of arrival by a hyphen. In the short form the departure square is omitted. The short form is used for describing

14

moves in this book.

A capture is written with an 'x' rather than a hyphen, so that ♖xg7 means a rook takes whatever piece occupies g7.

Castling kingside is denoted by 0-0, castling queenside by 0-0-0.

Here is an introductory game to show the notation in action. Start off with the pieces in the initial position and make the moves described below:

1	e4	e5
2	♘f3	♘c6
3	♗b5	♘f6
4	0-0	♘xe4
5	d4	♗e7
6	dxe5	0-0
7	♕d5	♘c5

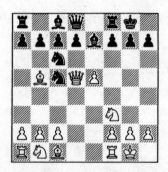

You should have reached the position in the diagram after making the seven moves written down.

Learning how to use the notation is very important if you want to learn about chess. All books have games written in chess notation, so you must learn it in order to be able to read chess books and magazines.

2 HOW TO CHECKMATE

The object of the game is to checkmate the opposing king and to make this possible it is usually necessary to have a superiority in forces. In order to checkmate the enemy king it is necessary to attack it and to ensure that it cannot move without moving into check.

As the king can move one square in any direction it is easier to bring about checkmate at the edge of the board, since fewer squares need to be controlled.

Some basic checkmates are described below:

KING AND QUEEN VERSUS KING

Let us start with the position in the diagram.

White has a king and queen and Black has a lone king; so White should have little trouble in checkmating the black king. This is best achieved by first driving the black king to the edge of the board, thereby limiting its movements, and then delivering checkmate itself:

1   ♕d6

The black king is limited to a small area from which he cannot escape; and White can now bring up his king to assist in the mating process.

In the ending it is important to use the king whenever possible.

1	...	♚f7
2	♔f2	♚e8
3	♔f3	♚f7
4	♔f4	♚g8
5	♕e7	

This limits the king to two squares: g8 and h8.

5	...	♚h8
6	♔g5	♚g8
7	♔g6	♚h8
8	♕e8 checkmate.	

The black king is checkmated. He is in check from the white queen and cannot move to g8, g7 or h7 because he could be captured there.

This should be an easy win for White . . .

. . .but he falls into the trap with ♕c7 – stalemate!

18

When playing an ending against a lone king, it is sometimes possible to give *stalemate* to your opponent, which means a draw. In the above example White has an easy win, but if he were to play the careless ♕c7 then Black would be stalemated, and the game drawn.

From the foregoing it can be concluded that stalemate occurs when the side who has the move cannot make one without moving his king onto a square which is attacked by an enemy piece. The black king cannot move to b8, b7 or a7 without being taken, but as his king is not already in check Black is stalemated and the game is a draw.

The correct procedure from the above position would have been:

1	♕h7	♚b8
2	♕d7	♚a8
3	♔g2	♚b8
4	♔f3	♚a8
5	♔e4	♚b8
6	♔d5	♚a8
7	♔c6	♚b8
8	♕b7 mate	('checkmate' abbreviated)

The black king cannot move to any square without being taken by the white queen, and cannot capture the white queen without being taken by the white king.

KING AND TWO ROOKS VERSUS LONE KING

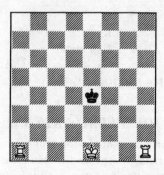

White has two rooks and a king versus a lone king.

1	♖h3

This limits Black to the fourth rank and beyond and prepares to further confine the black king.

1	...	♚f4
2	♖a4+	♚g5

Now the black king has been cut off from another rank by the white rooks. In order to drive the black king yet further back White must switch his rook over to the other side.

3	♖b3	♚f5
4	♖b5+	♚e6
5	♖a6+	♚d7
6	♖b7+	♚c8
7	♖h7	

Now the king is confined to the back rank and White will mate quickly.

7	...	♚b8
8	♖g6	♚c8
9	♖g8 mate.	

The mate with the two rooks is one of the easiest mates.

KING AND ROOK VERSUS KING

This is not such an easy mate as the king and queen versus king because the rook, being less powerful than the queen, needs more assistance from the king. In fact a lone rook, unlike a queen, will not even be able to drive the enemy king to the edge of the board unless it is helped by its own king.

| 1 | ♖f6 | |

The rook moves up to the sixth rank in order to restrict the black king to the last two ranks.

1	...	♚e7
2	♖a6	♚d7
3	♔f2	♚c7
4	♔e3	♚b7
5	♖h6	♚c7
6	♔d4	♚d7
7	♔e5	

An important move, bringing up the king to help.

Now if Black moves his king across to e7 then White can drive him to the back rank with ♖h7+. So the black king must flee to the queenside.

| 7 | ... | ♚c7 |
| 8 | ♔d5 | ♚b7 |

21

9	♔c5	♚a7
10	♔b5	♚b7
11	♖h7+	

White achieves his objective; the black king is forced to the back rank.

| 11 | ... | ♚c8 |
| 12 | ♔b6 | |

White does not directly oppose the black king, but instead moves to this square one file away from the king. The point of this is that Black cannot move 12 ... ♚b8 because of 13 ♖h8 mate and thus must keep moving his king across towards the white rook.

12	...	♚d8
13	♔c6	♚e8
14	♔d6	♚f8
15	♔e6	♚g8
16	♖f7	

Now the black king is restricted to h8 and g8.

16	...	♚h8
17	♔f6	♚g8
18	♔g6	♚h8
19	♖f8 mate.	

KING AND TWO BISHOPS VERSUS KING

The win is more difficult but the same principles apply: the king has to be driven to the back rank and mated in the corner.

How should White proceed? The first step is to limit the black king.

| 1 | ♗c4 | ♚e7 |

	2	♗b2

Now we can see that the black king is restricted to a triangle a3-a8-f8 by the two bishops. The white king has to assist the bishops in driving the king to the back rank.

	2	...	♚d6
	3	♔e2	♚c5
	4	♔d3	♚d6
	5	♗d4	

This further restricts the black king.

	5	...	♚c6
	6	♔e4	♚d6
	7	♔f5	♚c6
	8	♔e6	♚c7
	9	♗d5	♚d8
	10	♗c5	♚e8
	11	♗c6+	♚d8
	12	♔d6	♚c8

The black king is confined to the back rank; all that remains is to shepherd him into the corner being watchful for stalemate.

	13	♗b6	♚b8
	14	♗d5	♚c8
	15	♔c6	♚b8

The black king cannot escape and can only wait until White organises the final attack.

	16	♗e6	♚a8
	17	♗c5	♚b8
	18	♔b6	♚a8

Now the white king is in the correct position for checkmating the black king.

	19	♗e7	♚b8
	20	♗d6+	♚a8
	21	♗d5 mate.	

A useful tip in the mate with the two bishops is that the attacking king must be a knight's move away from the corner where the king is going to be mated.

We have seen examples of the various forces that can force checkmate against a lone king. In summary, here is a list of the *minimum* different forces needed, with the aid of the king, to force mate against a solitary king:

1) Queen
2) Rook
3) Two bishops
4) Knight and bishop.

Two knights cannot force mate though it is possible to mate if the opponent plays the defence incorrectly. If you have more material then in the summary above the mating procedure is made easier, though you must be careful to avoid stalemate.

It is essential to master these basic mates as, in serious tournaments, the rules state that you must administer mate in 50 moves when there are no pawns left on the board.

Thus we have seen that it is necesary to have a considerable advantage in forces before it is possible to checkmate. This might at first seem unlikely to occur in games between well matched opponents. But the lowly pawn is the key piece, particularly in the endgame, because when it reaches the eighth rank it can be promoted to any other piece (except a king). Thus a pawn could be promoted to a queen and this, in itself, would be sufficient with the aid of a king to force checkmate. Often an endgame is reached where one side has a king and a pawn and the other side has a lone king. The first point to consider is whether the lone king can stop the pawn.

Here White has an extra pawn which is far away from the black king. If White is to move he can queen the pawn.

1	h5	♚c8
2	h6	♚d8
3	h7	♚e8
4	h8♕+	

White is a queen up and will checkmate Black in due course.

Let us suppose that it is Black's move.

1	...	♚c8
2	h5	♚d8
3	h6	♚e8
4	h7	♚f8
5	h8♕+	

White still queens the pawn and wins the game, by bringing up his king to assist in checkmating the enemy king.

Let us change the original position slightly, so that the black king is one square closer to the pawn as in the diagram:

Now if it is White's turn to move he wins.

1	h5	♚d8
2	h6	♚e8
3	h7	♚f8
4	h8♕+	

But if it is Black's turn to move:

1	...	♚d8
2	h5	♚e8
3	h6	♚f8
4	h7	♚g7

Black stops the pawn from queening.

The next position is the same as the previous diagram, except that *the square of the pawn* has been drawn in. The square of the pawn can be found by drawing a line from the square the pawn occupies to the queening square, and then simply completing the square which has this line and the edges of the board as three of its sides.

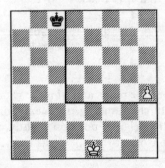

Here the black king stands just outside the square of the pawn. So from the diagram it can be appreciated that if it is Black's move he can enter the square and stop the pawn from queening, but if it is White's move Black cannot stop the pawn, since he cannot enter the square.

KING AND TWO PAWNS VERSUS KING

If one side has king and two pawns then the win is easier.

First, let us suppose that the pawns are on adjacent files.

White has no difficulty in winning this endgame as follows:

1	g5	♚g6
2	♔g4	♚g7
3	f5	♚f7
4	♔h5	♚g7
5	f6+	♚f7
6	♔h6	

26

As a general rule it is best to advance the king in front of the pawns.

6	...	♚g8
7	g6	♚h8
8	g7+	♚g8
9	f7+	♚xf7
10	♔h7	♚f6
11	g8♕	

and White wins.

Two separate pawns often win without the help of the king – the further the pawns are away from each other the more difficult for the lone king to stop both.

1	a4	♔e7
2	h4	♔e6
3	a5	

White is now threatening to play 4 a6 queening the a-pawn, so the black king has to move across to cover it.

3	...	♔d6
4 -	h5	

and White wins. Whichever way the black king moves, a white pawn promotes: if 4 .... ♔d5 5 h6 wins, or if 4 ... ♔e6 5 a6 wins.

KING AND PAWN VERSUS KING – THE OPPOSITION

We have seen that in some positions the king can stop a lone pawn if it is within range, but what happens if the attacking king is near? King and pawn versus king is a common and important ending and therefore before examining specific positions it is worth spending some time on the duel between two kings, known as the *opposition*.

The kings cannot move next to each other, otherwise they would be in check; the nearest approach is therefore where they are separated by one square.

fig 1 Vertical Opposition

In the diagram above the kings stand facing each other vertically in a position known as *vertical* opposition. They are blocking each other's way, for neither king can move to c4, d4 or e4.

fig 2 Horizontal Opposition

Here the kings stand facing each other horizontally in a position known as *horizontal* opposition and again they block each other's way to certain squares. Neither king can move to e3, e4 or e5.

fig 3 Diagonal Opposition

Here the kings stand facing each other diagonally in a position known as *diagonal* opposition.

Why are these positions important to understand? Because they hold the key to the battle for control of certain squares; whichever king has to move in these positions has to give way and let the opposing king gain certain squares.

In *fig 1*, if it is White to move Black has the opposition and White must give way.

	1	♔e3	♚c4

or

	1	♔c3	♚e4

In *fig 2*, if it is Black to move White has the opposition.

	1	...	♚d5
	2	♔e3	

or

	1	...	♚d3
	2	♔e5	

In *fig 3* the diagonal opposition can be converted into the horizontal or vertical opposition:

	1	...	♚e4
	2	♔e2	

White has the vertical opposition.

	1	♔f3	♚d3

Black has the horizontal opposition.

The key to these positions where the kings are facing each other one square apart is that the side *not* having the move has the opposition.

This is a typical winning position if White is to move:

| 1 | e7 | ♚f7 |

Forced.

| 2 | ♔d7 |

followed by 3 e8♕.

If it was Black to move he would draw by:

1	...	♚d8
2	e7+	♚e8
3	♔e6

Stalemate.

Here White wins by 1 ♔d7 followed by 2 e7 and 3 e8♕. He must not play 1 e7+ ♚e8 2 ♔e6 stalemate.

These two positions are the basic winning positions with a pawn on the sixth rank. These winning positions can normally be forced as long as the attacking king has the opposition and is at least one square in front of the pawn.

Here it is Black to move:

1	...	♚f6
2	♔d5	♚f5

If 2 ... ♚e7 3 ♔e5 and White gains further ground.

3	e4+	♚f6
4	♔d6!	

The vital move taking the opposition. 4 e5+ ♚e7 5 e6 ♚e8!
6 ♔d6 ♚d8 is a draw.

4	...	♚f7
5	e5	♚e8
6	♔e6	

Another important move taking the opposition. 6 e6 ♚d8
draws.

6	...	♚f8
7	♔d7	

and White wins.

There is an exception to this rule and that is with a rook's pawn:

1	...	♚h7
2	♔h5	♚g7
3	♔g5	♚h7
4	h4	♚g7
5	h5	♚h7
6	h6	♚h8
7	♔g6	♚g8
8	h7+	♚h8
9	♔h6	

Stalemate.

In the case of a rook's pawn, the defending king can never be driven out of the corner. Also, the rook's pawn sometimes cannot be promoted even if the defending king is not in the corner.

Here, although the the black king is not in the corner, the white king cannot escape.

1	♔h7	

Or 1 ♔h5 ♚f5.

2	...	♚f7
2	h5	♚f8
3	h6	♚f7
4	♔h8	♚f8
5	h7	♚f7

Stalemate.

KING AND TWO PAWNS VERSUS KING AND PAWN

This is another important type of ending which often occurs in practice.

Here White wins but not easily:

| 1 | ♚f6 | ♚d8 |

Now the best way to make progress is to sacrifice the pawn in order to gain the opposition.

2	d7	♚xd7
3	♚f7	♚d8
4	♚e6	♚c7
5	♚e7	♚c8

Black is forced away by the white king which cannot be prevented from capturing the black pawn.

6	♚d6	♚b7
7	♚d7	♚b8
8	♚xc6	♚c8

Now we have a winning position with king and pawn v king.

9	♚d6	♚d8
10	c6	♚c8
11	c7 and wins.	

Often the win is easier:

33

Here White wins quickly by:

1	♔f5	♚d7
2	♔e5	♚c7
3	♔e6	♚d8
4	♔d6	♚e8
5	♔c7	

Queening the d-pawn, or:

1	♔f5	♚d7
2	♔e5	♚e7
3	d6+	♚d7
4	♔d5	

followed by capturing Black's pawn.

We have covered some of the basic checkmate and simpler king and pawn endings in this chapter. The more complicated endings will be covered in chapter 7.

3 BASIC OPENINGS

A good general knows he must deploy all his forces swiftly in order to attain victory. Similarly, a chessplayer should develop his pieces as soon as possible. The whole army must be brought into the fray because single units will either be quickly destroyed or forced to retreat.

Here are four general rules which will help you to develop your pieces quickly and effectively and thus obtain a good position in the opening:

1) First advance a pawn in order to open up lines for the pieces to be developed.

2) Then bring out the knights and bishops. The knights are normally sent out before the bishops. As we have seen, the knight is not very powerful on the edge of the board but can be strong in the centre.

3) Castle. This puts the king in a safer position and prepares to develop the rooks.

4) Centralize the rooks and develop the queen. (The queen is valuable and should not be exposed too early to the enemy minor pieces and pawns.)

In this chapter we shall examine some straightforward openings and see how these general principles are applied in practice.

THE SCOTCH GAME

This is an aggressive and simple opening for White to play. It was called the Scotch Game after a correspondence match between Edinburgh Chess Club and London Chess Club in 1824.

1   e4

White advances a pawn to open a diagonal for the king's bishop and stakes a claim to the important central squares e4 and d5.

1   ...   e5

Similarly Black opens a diagonal for his king's bishop and attempts to control e5 and d4.

2   ♘f3

White develops his knight nearer the centre and also attacks the black pawn on e5. Thus 2 ♘f3 is not only a developing move but also an attacking move. A move such as this gains time since Black must now defend the pawn.

2   ...   ♘c6

Black defends his pawn on e5 and also brings out a knight.

3   d4

A vigorous move. White again attacks the pawn on e5 and opens up another diagonal, this time the diagonal for his queen's bishop. Black now has to decide whether to defend his pawn on e5 again or exchange on d4.

3   ...   exd4

The best move:

a) 3 ... d6 4 dxe5 ♘xe5 5 ♘xe5 dxe5 6 ♕xd8+ ♔xd8 7 ♗c4 is better for White since Black has lost the right to castle and must now waste time defending the f-pawn.

b) 3 ... ♘xd4 4 ♘xd4 exd4 5 ♕xd4 and it is difficult to drive the white queen from her dominating position in the centre.

c) 3 ... ♕e7 4 d5 ♘b8 5 c4 with a big space advantage to White.

4   ♘xd4   ♘f6

A good alternative is 4 ... ♗c5 5 ♗e3 ♕f6 6 c3 ♘ge7 with an equal game.

4 ... ♘f6 is a direct attack on the white e-pawn and a developing move; another example of an attacking and developing move.

5   ♘c3

Defending the pawn on e4 and bringing out the knight.

5 ... ♗b4

This is an example of a pin. The black bishop pins the white knight on c3 against the white king and thus Black threatens to take the white e-pawn with ... ♘xe4. The white knight could not recapture since the white king would then be in check.

6 ♘xc6

White wants to defend his e-pawn again by ♗d3 so he must exchange the knights first.

6 ... bxc6

If Black recaptures with the other pawn – 6 ... dxc6 7 ♕xd8+ ♔xd8 8 ♗d2 – then White has the advantage. The black king has lost the right to castle and Black cannot win the e-pawn since after 8 ... ♗xc3 9 ♗xc3 ♘xe4 10 ♗xg7 regains a pawn.

7 ♗d3 d5!

A good move. Black opens the diagonal for his queen's bishop and again threatens the white pawn on e4.

37

	8	exd5	cxd5
	9	0-0	0-0

Both sides castle quickly so as to remove their kings from the open e-file. Castling is very important as if the king is left in the centre he will be exposed to the enemy pieces.

10   ♗g5

An attacking move. This move is dangerous for Black if he does not realise that White has two threats:

Threat (1)   **11 ♗xf6 ♛xf6 12 ♘xd5 ♛xb2 13 ♖b1** winning the bishop on b4.

Threat (2)   **11 ♘xd5 ♛xd5 12 ♗xf6 gxf6 13 ♗xh7+ ♔xh7 14 ♛xd5** winning the black queen.

A good habit to acquire when playing a game is to check your opponent's move before you write it down for any threats.

10   ...   ♗e6

A good move stopping both threats and developing the bishop.

11   ♛f3

White brings out his queen putting more pressure on the black knight on f6 which is pinned by the white bishop on g5.

11   ...   ♗e7

Black brings the bishop back to protect the knight.

12   ♖fe1

White places the rook on the e-file where it is not obstructed by any pawns. Rooks are almost always better placed on files where there are no pawns obstructing their freedom of movement.

12   ...   ♖b8

The game is equal since both sides have developed their forces satisfactorily and have no weaknesses.

The Scotch Game is a direct opening and a good one to start with. Another similar opening is the Scotch Gambit which starts with the same moves.

1	e4	e5
2	♘f3	♘c6
3	d4	ed
4	♗c4	

But instead of recapturing the pawn White develops his king's bishop. A gambit is where one side sacrifices material (usually a pawn) hoping to get an advantage in development and position.

4 ... ♗c5

Black defends his pawn again and develops his king's bishop.

5 c3

The immediate attack on f7 does not lead to any advantage to White: 5 ♘g5 ♘h6 6 ♘xf7 ♘xf7 7 ♗xf7+ ♔xf7 8 ♕h5+ g6 9 ♕xc5 d5 10 ♕xd5+ ♕xd5 11 exd5 ♘b4 12 ♘a3 ♖e8+ 13 ♔d1 ♘xd5 with a better game for Black since he has an advantage in development.

5 ... dxc3

6 ♘xc3

White could regain his sacrificed pawn by 6 ♗xf7+ ♔xf7 7 ♕d5+ ♔f8 8 ♕xc5+ ♕e7 9 ♕xe7+ ♘gxe7 10 ♘xc3 but the game would then be equal since White's dangerous king's bishop has been exchanged.

6 ... d6

Black does not immediately develop his king's knight since White could gain time by attacking it: 6 ... ♘f6 7 e5 and the black knight is forced to worse square.

7 ♕b3

39

This line-up of the queen and bishop is dangerous for Black, who must defend the pawn on f7 or perish. He cannot do this with a knight since White will exchange the knight and then capture on f7, e.g. 7 ... ♞h6 8 ♗xh6 gxh6 9 ♗xf7+ or 7 ... ♞e5 8 ♞xe5 dxe5 9 ♗xf7+. Black can only defend the pawn with his queen.

> **7 ... ♛d7**

Why does Black put the queen here instead of on e7 of f6? The answer is that after ... ♛e7 or ... ♛f6 White can attack the queen with ♞d5.

Now Black threatens to exchange White's powerful king's bishop by ... ♞a5, attacking the white queen and bishop.

> **8 ♞d5**

White prevents ... ♞a5 for the following reason: 8 ... ♞a5 9 ♛c3 ♞xc4 10 ♛xg7 and the black rook on h8 perishes.

> **8 ... ♞ge7**
>
> **9 ♛c3**

Attacking g7. Now if Black plays 9 ... ♞xd5 White does not reply 10 exd5 because of 10 ... ♗b4 pinning and winning the queen. Instead White plays 10 ♛xg7 attacking the rook first.

> **9 ... 0-0**
>
> **10 0-0 ♞xd5**
>
> **11 exd5**

Now Black could retreat his knight to e7 – 11 ... ♞e7 – but after 12 b4 ♗b6 13 ♗b2 White has strong pressure on the long diagonal, and would threaten ♛xg7 checkmate.

> **11 ... ♞e5!**

12	♘xe5	exd5
13	♕xe5	♗d6

Black has given back his pawn in order to free his position. After White has moved his queen, Black can move his own queen and then develop his queen's bishop.

THE KING'S GAMBIT

1	e4	e5
2	f4	

Another simple and direct opening. White again puts pressure on the black pawn on e5 and offers a pawn to gain control of the centre.

| 2 | ... | exf4 |

Black can also decline the gambit with 2 ... ♗c5 or 2 ... d5.

| 3 | ♘f3 | |

The strongest move. White develops the knight where it controls the important central squares d4 and e5 and at the same time prevents a queen check on h4.

| 3 | ... | g5 |

An aggressive move. Black tries to hold on to the gambit pawn.

| 4 | h4 | |

White tries to break up the enemy pawns. If Black captures on h4 then White obtains the advantage: 4 ... gxh4 5 d4 ♗h6 6 ♖xh4 and Black is hard pressed.

4	...	g4
5	♘e5	

41

White is attacking the pawn on g4 and also threatening to play ♗c4 with a double attack on f7.

5 ... d5

Black stops ♗c4 and opens up the position for the queen's bishop.

6 d4

White ignores the attack on the e4 pawn. He can do this because after 6 ... dxe4 7 ♗c4 ♘h6 8 ♗xf4 he is threatening to capture on h6 and then invade on f7.

6 ... ♘f6

A good developing move which protects the pawn on g4 and puts pressure on e4 and d5.

7 ♗xf4 ♘xe4

8 ♘d2

White now threatens to exchange the knight on e4 and then play ♗c4 with a decisive attack on f7.

42

8	...	♘xd2
9	♕xd2	♗d6
10	0-0-0	♗e6
11	♗d3	

A typical gambit position. Black is a pawn up but White is ahead in development and has good play down the e-file and f-file.

THE FOUR KNIGHTS GAME

1	e4	e5
2	♘f3	♘c6
3	♘c3	♘f6
4	♗b5	

White develops his bishop with the threat ♗xc6 followed by ♘xe5.

4	...	♗b4

Black counterattacks rather than defending his e-pawn. 4 ... d6 defends the e-pawn but is passive since it blocks in the king's bishop. Now White cannot win a pawn by 5 ♗xc6 dxc6 6 ♘xe5 ♕e7 7 d4 because of 7 ... ♘xe4.

5	0-0	0-0
6	d3	

White opens the diagonal for his queen's bishop. Again 6 ♗xc6 dxc6 7 ♘xe5 ♖e8 8 ♘d3 ♗xc3 9 dxc3 ♘xe4 does not lead to advantage for White.

6	...	d6
7	♗g5	

43

Again this is an aggressive move. White's threat is 8 ♘d5 with a double attack on the black knight on f6. So Black exchanges off the dangerous knight.

| | 7 | ... | ♗xc3 |
| | 8 | bxc3 | ♕e7 |

This move needs explanation. White is preparing to play d4 attacking the pawn on e5, and ... ♕e7 defends this vital point. It also prepares to redeploy the black queen's knight via d8 to e6, where it will attack White's annoying bishop on g5.

9 ♖e1

White protects his e-pawn in preparation for d4. Indirectly the white rook threatens the black queen and Black must be careful not to let pawns be exchanged on the e-file, leaving his queen under attack.

| | 9 | ... | ♘d8 |
| | 10 | d4 | |

White achieves his projected advance d4. Black must not exchange on d4 since after 10 ... exd4 11 cxd4 White is threatening e5 winning a piece. Instead Black develops his last piece.

10 ... ♗g4

Both sides have completed their development. White has more space but Black has a solid game and long-term prospects because of the weakness of White's pawns on the c-file.

White will play his bishop on b5 back to d3 and his queen's rook to b1, while Black will complete his plan of bringing the knight to e6.

THE GIUOCO PIANO

The name *Giuoco Piano* is the Italian for 'quiet game'.

	1	e4	e5
	2	♘f3	♘c6
	3	♗c4	

This move strikes at the weakest point in the black position – f7. It can lead to quiet positions or violent attacks.

	3	...	♗c5
	4	c3	

White's idea is to build up a pawn centre with 5 d4. In the openings both sides aim to control the centre since, as we have seen, this is where the pieces are more powerful.

	4	...	♗b6

Black could also play 4 ... ♘f6 5 d4 exd4 6 cxd4 ♗b4+ 7 ♗d2 ♗xd2+ 8 ♘bxd2 d5 9 exd5 ♘xd5 with an equal game.

	5	d4	♕e7

Black defends his strong point on e5.

	6	0-0	d6
	7	h3	

White prevents Black from pinning the knight on f3 by ... ♗g4.

	7	...	♘f6

45

| 8 | ♖e1 | 0-0 |
| 9 | ♘a3 | |

White cannot develop his knight on d2 since 9 ... exd4 10 cxd4 ♘xd4 would win a pawn. White is planning to bring his knight to c4 after retreating his king's bishop.

Black has a solid position and will regroup his pieces either by ... ♘d8 or ... ♔h8 and ... ♘g8.

THE RUY LOPEZ

This is one of White's strongest openings. It is named after a Spanish priest who analysed it in 1561.

1	e4	e5
2	♘f3	♘c6
3	♗b5	

White is threatening to play at some point ♗xc6 followed by ♘xe5.

3	...	a6
4	♗a4	

White cannot yet win the e-pawn by 4 ♗xc6 dxc6 5 ♘xe5 because of 5 ... ♛d4 winning back the pawn.

4	...	♘f6

Black counter-attacks the white e-pawn.

5	0-0	♗e7

This is the *closed* variation of the Ruy Lopez. 5 ... ♘xe4 leads to the *open* variation which will be covered later.

6	♖e1	b5

White was threatening to capture the e-pawn now with 7 ♗xc6 dxc6 8 ♘xe5, when 8 ... ♛d4 is no good because of 9 ♘f3.

7	♗b3	d6
8	c3	

Again White prepares to build up a pawn centre with d4.

8	...	0-0
9	h3	

Before playing d4 White prevents Black from pinning the white knight with ... ♗g4.

9	...	♘a5

Black moves his knight to the edge of the board. Normally this is not a good idea but here Black has a specific purpose in mind. He wants to advance his c-pawn and obtain a queenside attack.

10	♗c2	c5
11	d4	♛c7

This is a more complicated position than any we have reached before. White will aim for an attack on the kingside and will transfer his queen's knight over there by ♘bd2, ♘f1 and ♘g3. Meanwhile Black will aim for counterplay on the queenside.

QUEEN'S GAMBIT, TARTAKOWER DEFENCE

	1	d4	d5
	2	c4	

The Queen's Gambit, unlike its violent counterpart the King's Gambit, is quiet and positional.

	2	...	e6

Black can also accept the gambit with 2 ... dxc4 3 ♘f3 ♘f6 4 e3 ♗g4 5 ♗xc4 e6 6 ♘c3 ♘bd7 with reasonable play, or alternatively 4 e3 e6 5 ♗xc4 c5, again with an equal game.

2 ... e6 is the Orthodox Defence to the Queen's Gambit. The drawback is that Black's queen's bishop is rather blocked in.

	3	♘c3	♘f6
	4	♗g5	

Again this pin is strong. White threatens 5 cxd5 exd5 6 ♗xf6 ♕xf6 7 ♘xd5.

	4	...	♗e7
	5	e3	0-0
	6	♘f3	h6
	7	♗h4	b6

The *Tartakower Defence*, in which Black prepares to 'fianchetto' his queen's bishop, is one of the best replies to the Queen's Gambit. A fianchetto is the development of a bishop on the square in front of the knight's original square.

8   cxd5

White captures on d5 rather than develop his king's bishop to d3. After 8 ♗d3 dxc4 9 ♗xc4 ♗b7 10 0-0 ♘e4 the game is equal.

8   ...   ♘xd5

Black recaptures with the knight in order to exchange pieces, thereby freeing his position.

9	♗xe7	♕xe7
10	♘xd5	exd5
11	♖c1	

White delays developing his kingside in order to position his rook on the half open file.

11   ...   ♗e6

A good move. The bishop is better placed here than on b7, since it exerts more influence on the kingside.

12   ♕a4

An unusual move in the opening but White wishes to answer a later ... c5 with ♕a3.

12   ...   c5

13   ♕a3

The black pawn on c5 is pinned; it cannot move without the black queen being captured by the white queen.

13   ...   ♖fc8

Defending the black pawn on c5 again.

14   ♗e2

White has a small advantage.

THE SLAV DEFENCE TO THE QUEEN'S GAMBIT

1	d4	d5
2	c4	c6
3	cxd5	cxd5
4	♘c3	♘f6
5	♘f3	♘c6
6	♗f4	e6

Black could also have continued with 6 ... ♗f5, but ... e6 is the safest move.

7	e3	♗e7
8	♗d3	0-0
9	h3	

White gives his bishop on f4 an escape square on h2. 9 0-0 ♘h5 10 ♗e5 f5 is satisfactory for Black.

9	...	♗d7
10	0-0	♕b6
11	♕e2	♖fc8
12	♖ac1	♗e8
13	♖fd1	♕d8

Black has a solid position.

4 BASIC TACTICS

After the opening comes the middlegame, both sides having developed their forces and castled. The aim of the game is to checkmate the enemy king but usually a straight attack is not possible. However, a superior force will eventually lead to a position where the enemy can be checkmated and in order to gain a suitable advantage in force or material there are a number of combinations or tactics available. These combinations can be divided into various types and are easily learned.

THE FORK

A fork is where one piece attacks two enemy pieces at the same time. Only one piece will be able to move and the other will be captured.

The simplest fork is the pawn fork.

Here the white pawn is threatening to capture both the black knight and the black rook. Black can move one of these away but the other one can then be captured.

THE KNIGHT FORK

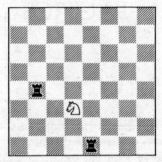

Here the white knight is attacking two black rooks.

THE BISHOP FORK

Here the black bishop is attacking three white pieces; two rooks and a knight.

THE ROOK FORK

The white rook is attacking two black bishops.

THE QUEEN FORK

The white queen is attacking the black knight and the black rook.

The fork is a powerful weapon and is generally most useful when a lesser piece is attacking more powerful pieces.

The most common are the pawn fork and knight fork. Here are some examples of the fork from actual play.

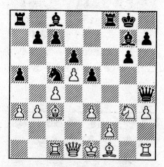

This position is from a game Larsen-Portisch at the Siegen Olympiad, 1970. Black now continued with . . .

1	...	♖xf2
2	♔xf2	♘e4+

This is a knight fork based on a pin. After 3 ♔g2 ♕xg3 is mate and 3 ♔e1 ♕xg3+ 4 ♔e2 ♕f2 is mate. White cannot capture the knight because he would be in check.

3	♔g1	♕xg3+
4	♗g2	♕xe3+

White resigned here because after 5 ♔h2 ♘xc3 Black has a big material advantage (knight, bishop and two pawns for a rook) and a better position.

This position is from the game Evans v Benko, played at Lone Pine, USA 1975. White exploited the strong position of his knights to win as follows:

1	♖xe6+	fxe6

If 1 ... ♖xe6 2 ♘xf5+ wins a piece.

2	♖xe6+	♖xe6
3	♘xf5+	♔c7
4	♘xe6+	♔d7
5	♘exg7	

White has a winning advantage with his two knights and pawn versus rook.

The position arose in Speelman v Povah, British Championship 1982.

White now leapt in with his knights.

1	♘b5!	♕c8

The black queen is forced to guard the bishop on b7.

54

	2	♘f5

Now White threatens ♘(either)d6+ and Black has no adequate defence. Black is forced to surrender his queen.

	2	...	♗xg2
	3	♘bd6+	♚d8
	4	♘xc8	♗xh1
	5	♘cd6	♗e4
	6	♘xf7+	♚e8
	7	♘7d6+	♗xd6
	8	♘xd6+	♚e7
	9	♘xe4	♘xe4
	10	♛d3	

White's material advantage forced Black to capitulate in a few moves.

Another good example of a knight fork is the following:

Black continued 1 ... ♖g2! and White resigned. Black is threatening 2 ... ♘f4 mate and White has no reasonable defence, e.g. (1... ♖g2) 2 ♚xg2 ♘e3+ followed by 3 ... ♘xd1; or 2 ♛c1 ♘f4+ 3 ♛xf4+ gxf4 4 ♚xg2 e5 and Black has a won pawn endgame.

THE PIN

This is another common form of tactic. The characteristics of a pin are that a piece prevents an enemy piece from moving because of a hidden attack on the piece of greater value.

The pin can easily be illustrated by some simple examples.

Here the white knight is pinned by the black bishop against the white queen. This has two effects: the white knight cannot move because the queen will be captured and the white queen is tied down to defending the knight.

This pin is not permanent since the knight can move. A permanent pin is where a piece is pinned against a king.

Here the white bishop pins the black knight against the black king and thus the knight can never move.

Why is the pin such a strong weapon? The pinned piece cannot move and thus if it can be attacked further it will fall.

Here the position is similar to the previous diagram except that White has a pawn on e2. He can move this to e4:

Now White wins the knight on d5. The pin is a very powerful weapon and we shall look at several different examples.

Here is a cautionary example of a pin:

Iskov-Bartrina
Olot (Spain) 1974

1	c4	♘f6
2	♘c3	e5
3	♘f3	♘c6
4	g3	g6
5	d4	exd4
6	♘xd4	♘e5
7	♗f4	♕e7
8	♘db5	

Black now mated White with 8 ... ♘f3 mate, exploiting the pin on the e-pawn.

Another game using this pin was Keres-Arlamowski, Bad Salzbrun 1950:

1	e4	c6
2	♘c3	d5
3	♘f3	dxe4
4	♘xe4	♘f6
5	♕e2	♘bd7??
6	♘d6 mate.	

This position is from a game Findlay-Williams, Paignton 1974. White now exploited the pin to win as follows:

1	♖xd4	♗xd4

Black resigned here because White will checkmate him with:

2	♕xa6+	

Black cannot capture the queen because of the pin.

2	...	♔b8
3	♕xb7 mate.	

This position, from Bronstein-Tal, Erevan (USSR) 1975 illustrates a cross pin.

White played 1 ♕d2 and Black is lost. He cannot capture the queen because the bishop is pinned against the king. If Black captures the bishop on b2 then White will capture the black queen with a decisive material advantage.

This is from a game Golombek-Wheatcroft, London 1937. Black now played the fine move 1 ... b5! The pin on the white knight prevents White from taking this pawn with his knight. 2 cxb5 c4 and 2 cxd5 c4 both win a piece for Black since the white queen on b3 and the white bishop on d3 are forked. This is a combination of both pin and fork.

A typical pin occurs in the Ruy Lopez:

1	e4	e5
2	♘f3	♘c6
3	♗b5	d6
4	d4	♗d7

Black stops his knight being pinned by the white bishop.

5	♘c3	♘f6
6	0-0	♗e7
7	♖e1	0-0

This opening line is known as the Tarrasch Trap after Tarrasch-Marco, Dresden 1892 where this first occurred.

8	♗xc6	♗xc6
9	dxe5	dxe5
10	♕xd8	♖axd8
11	♘xe5	♗xe4

Not 11 ... ♘xe4 12 ♘xc6 winning a piece.

12	♘xe4	♘xe4

White cannot capture the knight on e4 because of ... ♖d1+ and checkmate.

13	♘d3

The point of White's play is that the black knight is pinned against the black bishop.

13	...	f5
14	f3	♗c5+
15	♘xc5	

The best. If 15 ♔f1 ♗b6 16 fxe4 fxe4+ 17 ♘f4 g5 regains the piece.

15	...	♘xc5
16	♗g5	♖d5
17	♗e7	

White wins the exchange since if Black moves the rook to f7 then 18 c4 wins the knight on c5.

When a piece is pinned against the king it cannot move and is thus in an *absolute* pin. When a piece is pinned against a queen or rook, for example, the pinned piece may be able to move. This is especially important where a piece is pinned against a queen because normally one could not move the pinned piece for fear of loss of the queen. In some circumstances, however, such a pin *can* be broken.

In this position the white knight is pinned by the black bishop against the queen. But White can break the pin with advantage:

    1   ♘xe5   ♝xd1+

If 1 ... dxe5 2 ♕xg4 and White has won a pawn.

    2   ♗xf7+   ♚e7
    3   ♘d5 **mate!**

THE SKEWER

The fork is a simultaneous attack on two pieces whereas the *skewer* attacks them in sequence. The skewer is an attack along a rank, file or diagonal on which a valuable piece is threatened, must move and, after moving, exposes another piece to capture.

Here the white bishop is skewering the black queen and rook.

Study of a skewer by Stamma

White is a rook up but Black is threatening checkmate with ... ♖h1 and also to capture the rook on c4.

1	♖h4	♖xh4
2	♖a3+	♔c4
3	♖a4+	♔b5
4	♖xh4	

winning.

Mecking-Tan
Petropolis 1973

White played a combination involving checks and then a skewer.

1	♗xf7+	♔xf7
2	♖xc7+	♕xc7
3	♕h7+	

and White wins the queen and the game.

This last example also illustrates the power of a check. The enemy must answer a check in some way and the time can be used to gain material.

THE DISCOVERED ATTACK

The following trap occurs quite often:

Black cannot play 1 ... ♘xd4 2 ♘xd4 ♛xd4 because of 3 ♗xh7+ *discovering* an attack on the queen and winning it after:

3	...	♚xh7
4	♛xd4	

THE DECOY

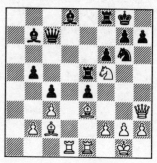

Blackburne-Steinitz
Vienna 1882

From this position White was able to force the win of material by:

| | 1 | ♖d7! | ♛xd7 |

Forced. If 1 ... ♛c8 2 ♖xg7+ ♚h8 3 ♛xh7 mate.

| | 2 | ♞h6+ | gxh6 |
| | 3 | ♛xd7 | |

White won with his material advantage.

This was an example of a *decoy* combination in which a piece is decoyed to a fatal square – in this case one where it could be won by a discovered attack.

Surprisingly White can win this position even though he only has bishop and two pawns against Black's queen, rook and pawn. He does this by a decoy combination.

| | 1 | ♗a7+ | |

1 bxc8♛+ ♚xc8 is lost for White.

| | 1 | ... | ♚xa7 |
| | 2 | bxc8♞+ | |

White promotes to a knight and duly forks the black king and queen.

	2	...	♚a6
	3	♞xe7	♚b6
	4	♚d5	♚a6
	5	♚e6	♚a7
	6	♚d7	♚b6
	7	♞d5+	

and White wins.

Clarke-de Veauce
Hastings 1971

White continued:

1	♕xh7+	♚xh7
2	♗d3+	♚g8
3	♖xc7	

White has won a pawn and duly went on to win the game.

DISCOVERED AND DOUBLE CHECK

We now move on to these types of checks, which are very powerful weapons. We shall start off with a famous game played in Vienna back in 1908 which illustrates the power of a double check.

Réti-Tartakower
Vienna 1908

| 1 | e4 | c6 |

This is the Caro-Kann Defence.

2	d4	d5
3	♘c3	dxe4
4	♘xe4	♘f6
5	♕d3	e5
6	dxe5	♕a5+
7	♗d2	♕xe5
8	0-0-0	

Now Black cannot take the white knight with his queen – after 8 ... ♕xe4 9 ♖e1 pins and wins the queen.

8	...	♘xe4
9	♕d8+!	

The bombshell.

9	...	♚xd8
10	♗g5+	

The deadliest weapon on the chessboard – the double check – is unleashed (the rook on d1 and the bishop on g5 now both attack the enemy king which must move).

10	...	♚c7

10 ... ♚e8 11 ♖d8 mate.

11	♗d8 mate.	

Ed Lasker-Sir George Thomas
London 1913

In the above position Lasker sacrifices his queen for a discovered and double check.

1	♕xh7+	♚xh7

2	♘xf6+	♚h6

2 ... ♚h8 3 ♘g6 checkmate.

3	♘eg4+	♚g5

The black king is forced into the white camp where it will be surrounded quickly by the white pieces.

4	h4+	♚f4
5	g3+	♚f3
6	♗e2+	♚g2
7	♖h2+	♚g1
8	0-0-0 mate.	

Torre-Em. Lasker
Moscow 1925

Here White sets up a discovered check battery by sacrificing his queen.

1	♗f6	♛xh5
2	♖xg7+	♚h8
3	♖xf7+	♚g8
4	♖g7+	♚h8
5	♖xb7+	♚g8

Black can do nothing but move his king while White gobbles up material.

6	♖g7+	♚h8
7	♖g5+	♚h7
8	♖xh5	♚g6

White has regained his queen but Black will be able to win back a bishop because his king is forking two pieces.

9	♖h3	♚xf6
10	♖xh6+	

White duly won with his extra pawns.

67

Reshevsky-Shainswit
New York 1951

A similar example, which this time leads to mate.

1	♖f3	e4?
2	♖xg3	exd3
3	♖xg7+	♔h8
4	♖xf7+	♔g8
5	♖g7+	♔h8
6	♖g3+	

Black cannot prevent mate.

One type of discovered check which is worth knowing is the technique leading to a smothered mate.

White wins by:

1	♕d5+	♔h8
2	♘f7+	♔g8

2 ... ♖xf7 3 ♕d8+ and mates next move.

3	♘h6++	♔h8
4	♕g8+	♖xg8

Forced.

5	♘f7 mate.

BACK RANK MATES

The basic idea is illustrated by this diagram. If it is White to move he can checkmate Black by 1 ♖e8 mate. If it is Black's move he can create an escape for his king on h7 by 1 ... h6.

This idea of checkmate on the back rank often turns up in more complicated form.

Bernstein-Capablanca
Moscow 1914

White now decided to capture the dangerous black pawn on c3 ...

1	♘xc3	♘xc3
2	♖xc3	♖xc3
3	♖xc3	

69

but now he was surprised by a remarkable move:

3 ... ♛b2!!

White cannot capture the queen with 4 ♕xb2 because of 4 ... ♖d1 mate, and if 4 ♖d3 ♕b1+ 5 ♕f1 ♕xf1+ 6 ♔xf1 ♖xd3 wins a rook and the game for Black.

Réti-Bogoljobow
New York 1924

White finished off the game as follows:

1 ♗f7+ ♔h8
2 ♗e8!

and Black resigned because of the possible continuations:

a) 2 ... ♖xe8 3 ♕xf8+ and mates.

b) 2 ... h6 3 ♕xf8+ and wins.

c) 2 ... ♗xc5+ 3 ♕xc5 ♖xe8 4 ♖f8+ and mates.

Here is another example where the lack of a bolt-hole for the king leads to mate:

Alekhine-Freeman
New York 1934

In this position White played a combination to exploit the weakness of Black's back rank.

    1   Ωe8+   ©f8

    2   ©h6+!

White exploits the pin of the g-pawn by his queen. Black cannot move his king into the corner because Ωxf8 is then mate.

    2   ...   ♛xh6

    3   Ωxf8+   ♔xf8

    4   ♛d8 mate.

Adams-Torre
New Orleans 1920

This position is famous for the play based on the weakness of the back rank. At the moment the black rook on e8 is securely protected by the black rook on c8 and the black queen on d7. If White can deflect either of these pieces from the defence of e8 he will be able to mate Black with Ωxe8+.

    1   ♛g4!

White can offer the queen since 1 ... ♛xg4 is met by 2 Ωxe8+ and mates. If 1 ... Ωxe2 2 ♛xd7 Ωxe1+ 3 ©xe1 Ωc1 4 ♔f1 wins for White, so Black must move his queen.

    1   ...   ♛b5

Black threatens 2 ... ♛xe2 3 Ωxe2 Ωc1+ followed by mate.

    2   ♛c4!

Stopping Black's threat and attacking the black queen again. Neither the black rook or queen can take the queen on c4 without allowing mate on e8.

    2   ...   ♛d7

    3   ♛c7!   ♛b5

4   a4

White can play this move now as 4 ... ♛xe2 5 ♜xe2 ♜xe2 6 ♛xc8 is mate.

4   ...   ♛xa4

5   ♜e4!

Another strong move. 5 ... ♛xe4 6 ♜xe4 ♜xe4 7 ♛xc8+ leads to mate, as does 5 ... ♜xe4 6 ♛xc8+.

5   ...   ♛b5

Black must keep protecting e8.

6   ♛xb7

Black resigned as his queen has no squares where it can guard e8.

STALEMATE

Stalemate occurs when a player is not in check but is unable to move (see pp 18-19). Thus the game ends in a draw.

Pilnik-Reshevsky
U.S. Championship 1942

Here Black is three pawns up and it would appear that he has an easy win, but there is a stalemate possibility which White discovers.

1   ♛f5   g4

If 2 ♛xg4 ♛e1+ 3 ♚g2 ♛g3+ exchanging queens, then Black wins White's last pawn with his king.

2   ♛f2

Pinning the black queen against the black king. Black must capture the queen.

2   ...   ♛xf2

Stalemate!

White is stalemated – his pawn cannot move and his king has no legal move.

Marshall-MacClure
New York 1923

White escaped to a draw as follows:

1	♖h6!	♖xh6

Forced.

2	h8♕+	♖xh8

Again forced.

3	b5

Now unless Black plays 3 ... ♖d7 White is stalemated.

3	...	♖d7
4	cxd7	c6?

White was threatening 5 d8♕ with a stalemate after ♖xd8, but after this blunder Black loses.

5	bxc6	♔b8
6	♔xb6	

and White wins!

PERPETUAL CHECK

Perpetual check is where one side keeps on giving check, and the other side cannot avoid it. Such games are drawn.

Here is a remarkable example.

Hamppe-Meitner
Vienna 1869

1	e4	e5
2	♘c3	♗c5

73

3   ♘a4   ♝xf2+

Black sacrifices his bishop to expose the enemy king.

4   ♔xf2   ♛h4+

Now White cannot play 5 g3 because of 5 ... ♛xe4 forking the knight on a4 and the rook on h1, nor 5 ♔e2 because of 5 ... ♛xe4+ forking the king and knight.

5   ♔e3   ♛f4+

6   ♔d3   d5

A good move opening up the diagonal for his queen's bishop. White cannot take the pawn because of his unprotected knight.

7   ♔c3   ♛xe4

8   ♔b3   ♘a6

Black threatens 9 ... ♛b4 mate.

9   a3   ♛xa4+!

A surprising queen sacrifice to drive the king further forward.

10   ♔xa4   ♘c5+

11   ♔b4   a5+

Again the king is forced forward – if 12 ♔c3 d4+.

12   ♔xc5   ♘e7

Black is threatening 13 ... b6+ 14 ♔b5 and 14 ... ♝d7 mate – White must try to prevent this.

13   ♝b5+   ♔d8

14   ♝c6

The only way to prevent checkmate. If Black now captures the bishop the white king is safe.

14   ...   b6+

15   ♔b5   ♘xc6

Black threatens 16 ... ♘d4+ 17 ♔a4 b5 mate.

16   ♔xc6   ♝b7+

Now if White captures the bishop he is checkmated by 17 ♔xb7 ♚d7 18 ♕g4+ ♚d6 and White cannot prevent 19 ... ♖hb8 mate.

17	♔b5	♗a6+
18	♔c6	

18 ♔a4 b5 mate.

18	...	♗b7+

The game is drawn by perpetual check after 19 ♔b5 ♗a6+.

OVERLOADING

A piece is overloaded when it has too many tasks to perform.

The black pawn on d6 performs too many tasks; it defends the knight on c5 and the bishop on e5. White can take advantage of this fact to win material.

1	♗xc5	dxc5
2	♖xe5	

UNDERMINING

Here the black rook is protected by the black knight which is in turn protected by the black pawn.

White undermines the black rook by capturing the black knight first.

1	♗xd5	exd5
2	♗xf4	

5 COMBINATIONS AND ATTACKS

In Chapter 3 some basic opening rules were introduced and the importance of developing all your pieces was pointed out. In Chapter 4 basic tactics were introduced. In this chapter we shall consider what happens if development of the pieces is neglected or the safety of the king is not attended to. Then we shall move on to attacks against the castled king and then finally to combinations.

We shall begin with a game which illustrates the importance of developing the pieces and moving the king to a safe haven.

Nimzowitsch-Alapin
USSR 1913
French Defence

1	e4	e6
2	d4	d5
3	♘c3	♘f6
4	exd5	♘xd5
5	♘f3	c5
6	♘xd5	♛xd5
7	♗e3	cxd4
8	♘xd4	

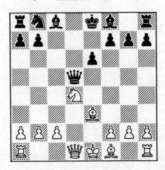

White has already developed two of his pieces whereas Black only has his queen in play.

8	...	a6
9	♗e2	

White offers his g-pawn which Black cannot decline.

9	...	♛xg2
10	♗f3	

White has lost a pawn but is ahead in development.

10	...	♛g6
11	♛d2	

White prepares to castle on the queenside and bring his rooks into the game.

11	...	e5

Black still neglects his development.

White now decides to offer the sacrifice of a piece in order to attack the black king down the central files.

12	0-0-0	exd4
13	♗xd4	

Now the black king is wide open down the centre files and no pieces are defending the monarch.

13	...	♞c6
14	♗f6!!	

Another stunning sacrifice. White threatens 15 ♛d8+ ♞xd8 16 ♖xd8 mate.

14	...	♛xf6
15	♖he1+	♗e7
16	♗xc6+	

Black cannot capture this bishop because of 17 ♛d8 mate.

16	...	♔f8
17	♕d8+!	♗xd8
18	♖e8 mate.	

An instructive game. Black did not develop his pieces and lost time with his queen in taking the white g-pawn, and consequently White was able to build up a very strong attack.

Here is another example, a game between two strong players, showing the dangers of neglected development and queen sorties early in the game.

Belyavsky-Stean
Lucerne Olypiad 1982
Sicilian Defence

1	e4	c5
2	♘f3	d6
3	d4	cxd4
4	♘xd4	♘f6
5	♘c3	a6
6	♗g5	e6
7	f4	♕b6

Black brings his queen out early; a dangerous policy.

8	♕d2	♕xb2
9	♘b3	

White has sacrificed a pawn but has compensation because he is ahead in development. Black will have to spend time retreating his queen.

9	...	♘bd7
10	♗d3	b5
11	0-0	♘c5?

This offer to exchange pieces is a decisive mistake – White now wins by a forced tactical sequence.

12	♘xc5	dxc5
13	♖ab1	♕a3
14	♗xf6	gxf6
15	♘xb5!	

Black resigned since after 15 ... axb5 16 ♗xb5+ ♔e7 17 ♖fd1 mate on d6, d7 or d8 cannot be prevented.

Here is another illustration of the importance of developing the pieces quickly and bringing the king to a safe haven. In this game between two grandmasters White sacrifices a piece to keep the opposing king in the centre.

Uhlmann-Ljubojević
Niksic 1978
English Opening

1	c4	c5
2	♘f3	g6
3	d4	♗g7
4	e4	cxd4
5	♘xd4	♘c6
6	♗e3	d6
7	♘c3	a6

White has more space and is slightly ahead in development. Black's last move was not necesary, and therefore 7 ... ♘f6, developing the knight and preparing to castle, was safer.

| 8 | ♗e2 | e6 |

This move is a definite mistake. Black should have developed his knight 8 ... ♘f6 with a view to castling. In the opening it is important not to make too many pawn moves, but to develop the pieces quickly.

$$9 \quad \text{♕d2} \qquad \text{♘e5}$$

This is another risky move .It is often bad to move the same piece twice in the opening, since it can lead to a position in which the other side has an advantage in development.

$$10 \quad \text{♖d1} \qquad \text{♕c7}$$

Black is a long way behind in development. White has six pieces in play – knights on c3 and d4, bishops on e2 and e3, the queen on d2 and a rook on d1, whereas Black has only three – a knight on e5, a bishop on g7 and the queen on c7. White is now able to sacrifice a piece in order to strand the black king in the centre.

$$11 \quad \text{♘db5} \qquad \text{axb5}$$
$$12 \quad \text{♘xb5}$$

Black must move his queen and allow White to capture the pawn on d6 with his knight, giving check.

$$12 \quad \text{...} \qquad \text{♕c6}$$
$$13 \quad \text{♘xd6+} \qquad \text{♔e7}$$
$$14 \quad \text{♕b4}$$

81

White now threatens a deadly discovered check with the knight, so the black king hurries away.

	14	...	♔f6
	15	f4	

White threatens to take the knight with check; if the knight moves White still wins, e.g. 15 ... ♘d7 16 e5+ ♘xe5 17 fxe5+ ♔xe5 18 ♕c3 mate.

	15	...	g5
	16	fxe5+	♔g6

Or 16 ... ♔xe5 17 ♕c3 mate.

	17	♘xf7	
		1-0	

If Black takes the knights on f7 he is checkmated by 18 ♗h5. If he does not take the knight, White will simply take the rook on h8 with a decisive advantage in material.

One of the weakest points in the initial position is f2 or f7. This point is only protected by the king. It is the least guarded point around the king. Disaster can befall the player who is not alert for threats against this square.

	1	e4	e6
	2	d4	d5
	3	♘d2	c5
	4	exd5	exd5
	5	dxc5	♗xc5

This is a standard opening position from the Tarrasch Variation of the French Defence. Note that the black king's bishop is aiming at the weak point on f2. If White plays the

blunder

> 6 ♘e2?

he is lost after

> 6   ...   ♛b6

Black has double attack on the weak point on f2. In fact he is threatening ... ♝xf2 mate; White cannot avoid losing a piece. For example, after 7 ♘b3 or 7 ♘f3, 7 ... ♝xf2+ 8 ♔d2 ♕e3 is mate. 7 ♘g3 ♝xf2+ 8 ♔e2 ♕e3 is also mate. White must play 7 ♘d4 ♝xd4 with an easy win for Black with his extra piece.

In these examples we have seen how vulnerable the king is in the middle of the board, so it is wise to castle quickly.

Let us consider the position after Black has castled kingside:

In this position, the vulnerable point f7 is defended by the black rook but the points g7 and h7 are only defended by the black king.

We are now going to consider attacks on a castled king position. The point h7 can be attacked in a number of ways:

1) By queen and bishop.

If it is White to move he can mate by ♕xh7.

2) By queen and knight.

If it is White to move he can checkmate by ♕xh7.

3) By queen and rook.

If it is White to move he can checkmate by ♕xh7.

4) By queen and pawn.

If it is White to move he can checkmate by ♕xh7.

The point g7 can also be attacked in a number of ways:
1) By queen and bishop.

In both positions if it is White to move he can checkmate Black by ♕xg7.

2) By queen and knight.

If it is White to move he can checkmate by ♕xg7.

85

3) By queen and rook.

If it is White's move he can checkmate by ♕xg7.

4) By queen and pawn.

If it is White to move he can checkmate Black by ♕xg7.

The basic attacks on the castled king are the key to many mating combinations in the middlegame.

The king's position is normally strongest when the pawns around it are unmoved. When the pawns are moved weak squares are created, which can be invaded by the enemy pieces.

Here the squares f6 and h6 are weak and can be used by the enemy, whilst if the f- or h-pawns are advanced one square they become a target for attack.

Consequently if you are attacking it is desirable to provoke weaknesses in the enemy king position; conversely, if you are defending, it is best to avoid moving the pawns around your king.

Here Black has a knight defending the king's position (the knight on f6 defends the vulnerable point on h7).

Now we shall look at some examples of attacks on the castled king.

White is attacking the black king and has an advanced pawn on g6. If the white queen was on h5 she could mate by ♕xh7 (similar to our previous example of a queen and pawn attack on h7). So White needs to get the queen to the h-file with gain of time. He does this by

1   ♖h8+

A decoy sacrifice by which White forces the black king to h8.

1	...	♔xh8
2	♖h1+	♔g8
3	♖h8+	

Another decoy sacrifice.

3	...	♔xh8
4	♕h1+	

The white queen has reached the h-file with gain of time and Black has had no time to organise a defence because of the checks.

4	...	♔g8
5	♕h7 mate.	

In this example the black h-pawn was missing, but the absence of any pawns in front of a king can lead to a quick mate.

Abrahams-Winter
London 1946

This game illustrates a number of mating positions arising from the advance of the g-pawn. White won by the surprising

1 ♗f8!

White threatens to mate Black on his next move by 2 ♕g7. But if Black captures the bishop with the rook – 1 ... ♖xf8 – then 2 ♘e7 is mate; if Black captures the bishop with the king – 1 ... ♔xh8 – then 2 ♕h8 is mate.

In the next position White has just played his rook to d5 and is now threatening to take the bishop on f1. If Black now retreats the bishop, then White can checkmate the black king: 1 ... ♗h3 2 ♕xh7+! ♔xh7 3 ♖h5 mate. This is another example where the absence of a pawn around the castled king leads to checkmate.

88

Lengyel-Sliwa
Altheide 1966

From this position White can checkmate Black as follows:

    1   **h6+**   ♔g8

    2   **♕f6**

and Black cannot prevent mate.

There are a number of combinations involving the sacrifice of a piece in order to expose the enemy king to a mating attack.

89

Here White has driven away Black's knight from the defence of the vulnerable point h7. He now sacrifices a piece to remove the black h-pawn and to expose the black king to a mating attack.

1	♗xh7+	♔xh7
2	♘g5+	♔g8
3	♕h5	

White now threatens ♕h7 mate.

3	...	♖e8
4	♕xf7+	♔h8
5	♕h5+	♔g8
6	♕h7+	♔f8
7	♕h8+	♔e7
8	♕xg7 mate.	

This is a standard sacrifice against a king position.

Here White can win by the simple

1	♗xg7	♔xg7
2	♕f6+	♔g8
3	♖g3 mate	

or the elegant

1	♕f6	gxf6
2	♖g3+	♔h8
3	♗xf6 mate.	

(See next diagram)

In this position White played a combination which won material.

Minić-Bukić
Yugoslavia 1967

1   ♖e8+

This move depends on an *overload* combination. If the black rook captures the white rook 1 ... ♖xe8 White captures the queen 2 ♕xd5 with a winning material advantage. The black rook is overloaded since it has to defend e8 as well as d5. However, Black has another reply:

1   ...   ♗f8

But now White wins a rook by

2   ♕xd5   ♖xd5
3   ♖xa8

In this position White won by a combination involving a pin.

1   ♖d1

Black cannot capture the rook because the queen is pinned.

1   ...   ♕xc4

> 2 **♖xd8+**

This is an in-between move sometimes called a *zwischenzug*.

> 2 ... **♔g7**
> 3 **bxc4**

White is a rook ahead.

Black wins by a combination involving a checkmate.

> 1 ... **♕xg4**

Black sacrifices the queen for the white rook which is protecting g2.

> 2 **fxg4** **♖xg2+**
> 3 **♔h1** **♖h2+**
> 4 **♔g1** **♖bg2 mate**

In this position White carries out a combination to expose the black king.

> 1 **♗xh7+** **♔xh7**
> 2 **♕h5+** **♔g8**

92

3	♗xg7

White strips the black king of his defensive barrier.

3	...	♚xg7
4	♕g5+	♚h8
5	♖d4	f6
6	♖h4+	♕h7
7	♖xh7+	♚xh7
8	♕h5+	♚g7
9	♖xe6	

with a winning advantage for White.

There are a number of combinations which revolve around the queening of a pawn.

Here Black wins by

1	...	♖a3+
2	♔d2	♖xf3
3	gxf3	h3

and White cannot stop the pawn from queening.

93

White concludes the game by giving up his queen.

> 1 ♕xd6+ ♕xd6
> 2 c7

and Black cannot stop the pawn queening without giving up his queen for it.

6 POSITIONAL PLAY

We have seen some basic tactics and attacks against the king, which are a major part of chess, but although such techniques are suitable for certain situations, how should one play if there are no combinations or possibilities of attack available? Well, it happens that chess can be played in a logical way, according to *the position*; it is important to know how to play positionally, and it is important to know how to plan. In some positions it is possible to play for an attack on one side of the board if the enemy has few pieces there.

As we have seen, control of the central squares is important since pieces are at their most powerful when placed in the centre.

It is unwise to attack on the flank if the centre is not blocked and the opponent can start an attack there. This point is illustrated in the following game:

Botvinnik-Capablanca
AVRO 1938

1	d4	♘f6
2	c4	e6
3	♘c3	♗b4
4	e3	

Black has played the Nimzo-Indian Defence and White prepares to develop his king's bishop on d3 controlling e4.

4	...	d5
5	a3	♗xc3+
6	bxc3	c5
7	cxd5	exd5

White now has the two bishops and his aim is to advance in the centre with f3 and e4.

8	♗d3	0-0
9	♘e2	b6
10	0-0	♗a6

11	♗xa6	♘xa6
12	♗b2	♕d7
13	a4	♖fe8
14	♕d3	

White is attacking the black knight and now Black decides to advance his c-pawn and attack on the queenside.

| 14 | ... | c4 |

Black hopes to manoeuvre his knight to b3 via b8, c6 and a5, and then attack the white a-pawn. This strategy is incorrect because White can break through with an attack in the centre.

15	♕c2	♘b8
16	♖ae1	♘c6
17	♘g3	♘a5
18	f3	♘b3
19	e4	♕xa4

Black has succeeded in capturing the white a-pawn with his

queenside attack, but White has a big central position which he can use to drive back the enemy forces.

20	e5	♘d7
21	♕f2	

White transfers the queen to the kingside in readiness for an attack on the black king.

21	...	g6
22	f4	f5

Black tries to block the white attack.

23	exf6	♘xf6
24	f5	♖xe1
25	♖xe1	♖e8

Black hopes to blunt the force of White's attack by exchanging pieces.

26	♖e6	♖xe6
27	fxe6	

White's central attack has resulted in a strong passed pawn.

27	...	♔g7
28	♕f4	

The white queen threatens to invade the black position.

28	...	♕e8
29	♕e5	♕e7

Black appears to have defended successfully but now White has a decoy sacrifice drawing the black queen away from the defence of the kingside.

30	♗a3!	♕xa3
31	♘h5+	gxh5
32	♕g5+	♔f8

33	♛xf6+	♚g8
34	e7	

Now Black cannot stop the pawn from queening and must hope for a perpetual check.

34	...	♛c1+
35	♚f2	♛c2+
36	♚g3	♛d3+
37	♚h4	♛e4+
38	♚xh5	♛e2+
39	♚h4	♛e4+
40	g4	♛e1+
41	♚h5	

Black resigned since he has no defence to the threat of ♛f8.

So it is important not to neglect the centre in order to attack on the flank. It is possible to start a flank attack without fear if the centre is completely blocked.

Larsen-Fischer
Candidates Match 1971

1	c4	g6
2	♘f3	♗g7
3	d4	♘f6
4	♘c3	0-0
5	e4	d6
6	♗e2	e5
7	0-0	♘c6
8	d5	♘e7
9	♘d2	c5

The centre is blocked and now both sides commence attacks on the flank. White will attack on the queenside and Black on the kingside.

10	♖b1	♞e8
11	b4	b6
12	a4	f5
13	a5	♞f6
14	♕a4	♝d7
15	♕a3	♝h6
16	♝d3	♕c7
17	bxc5	bxc5
18	exf5	

This is a mistake. White should not open up the g-file which Black can use to attack the white king.

| 18 | ... | gxf5 |
| 19 | ♝c2 | a6 |

Black prevents a white knight jumping in on b5.

20	♞de4	♝xc1
21	♞xf6+	♖xf6
22	♖fxc1	♖af8

Black transfers all of his pieces to the kingside ready for an attack there.

| 23 | ♖b6 | |

A blow in the dark; the threat of ♖xa6 is easily parried. Better was 23 ♕b3 with the idea of penetrating with the queen.

23	...	♝c8
24	♞e2	f4
25	♝e4	♞f5

99

26	♖c6	♕g7

Black now has concentrated all of his forces on the white king and there is no defence.

27	♖b1	♘h4
28	♕d3	♗f5

Setting up a dangerous pin; Black threatens ... ♘xg2.

29	♔h1	f3
30	♘g3	fxg2+
31	♔g1	♗xe4
32	♕xe4	♘f3+
33	♔xg2	♘d2

White resigned because he not only loses the exchange but the pawn on f2.

In the above diagram, the white pawns on c2 and c3 are *doubled isolated* pawns; the pawn on a5 is *isolated*, as is the black pawn on h4. The white pawn on g2 and the black one on b7 are *backward* pawns. The black pawns on e5 and f5 are called *hanging* pawns.

Isolated pawns, which are separated from other pawns by at least one file, can be a liability since they need to be defended by pieces. The following instructive game illustrates the weakness of such a pawn.

Fischer-Petrosian
Candidates Match 1971

1	e4	c5
2	♘f3	e6
3	d4	cxd4
4	♘xd4	a6

5	♗d3	♘c6
6	♘xc6	bxc6
7	0-0	d5
8	c4!	

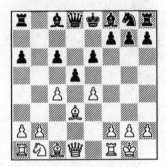

White attacks the black pawn centre, hoping to break it up leaving Black with an isolated pawn.

8	...	♘f6
9	cxd5	cxd5
10	exd5	exd5

The alternative 10 ... ♘xd5 11 ♗e4 is awkward for Black.

11	♘c3	♗e7
12	♕a4+	♕d7

Black offers the exchange of queens, but this allows White to obtain a grip on the position. 12 ... ♗d7 was better.

13	♖e1	

This forces Black to exchange queens.

13	...	♕xa4
14	♘xa4	♗e6
15	♗e3	0-0

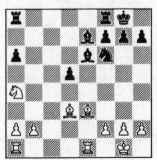

101

Black is tied down to the defence of his d-pawn and the pawn on a6.

	16	♗c5	♖fe8
	17	♗xe7	♖xe7
	18	b4	

This is a good positional move. White effectively fixes the black pawn on a6 because if Black advances it White can reply b5 with a srong passed pawn.

	18	...	♔f8
	19	♘c5	♗c8
	20	f3	

This allows White to bring his king to the centre via f2.

	20	...	♖7a7
	21	♖e5	♗d7
	22	♘xd7+	

White exchanges his knight for the black bishop since his remaining minor piece, the bishop, is much superior to the black knight.

	22	...	♖xd7
	23	♖c1	

White takes control of the open c-file. It is important to place rooks on open files.

	23	...	♖d6
	24	♖c7	♘d7
	25	♖e2	

Black is almost completely tied down. The black knight cannot move since then White would invade with ♖ee7 attacking f7.

	25	...	g6

| 26 | ♔f2 | h5 |
| 27 | f4 | h4? |

Now this pawn is cut off from the rest of the black army and White can attack it with his king.

| 28 | ♔f3 | |

The white king is threatening to round up the pawn with ♔g4.

| 28 | ... | f5 |
| 29 | ♔e3 | |

Now the white king is threatening to come to a commanding post on d4.

29	...	d4+
30	♔d2	♘b6
31	♖ee7	

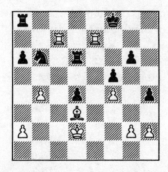

White now has doubled rooks on the seventh rank and these exert tremendous power.

31	...	♘d5
32	♖f7+	♔e8
33	♖b7	♘xb4
34	♗c4	

Black resigned in this position since he has no defence to 35 ♖h7 ♖f6 36 ♖h8+ ♖f8 37 ♗f7+ ♔d8 38 ♖xf8 mate.

This game showed the weakness of isolated pawns. Black was tied down to the defence of his pawns on a6 and d5. Another feature was the power of two rooks on the seventh rank.

In the next example a pure rook ending has been reached, but White has much the stronger pawns. Black has isolated doubled pawns on the a-file, an isolated d-pawn and doubled pawns on the

Taulbut-Perkins
Borehamwood 1981

g-file, whereas White has only a backward b-pawn. White was able to capture the weak black pawns as follows:

1	♖ad1	♖ab8
2	♖d2	

White can afford to defend his b-pawn as Black must contend with the threat of ♖e5.

2	...	♖b6
3	♖e5	♖fb8
4	♖exd5	♖xb2
5	♖xb2	♖xb2
6	♖xg5	♖c2
7	♖xa5	♖xc3
8	♖xa6	

White is now two pawns up and he converted this into a win as follows:

104

8	...	♖a3
9	♔g2	g5
10	♖a5	f6
11	♖a7	

This ties the black king down to the back rank.

| 11 | ... | ♔f8 |
| 12 | h4 | |

White forces another passed pawn on the kingside.

12	...	gxh4
13	gxh4	♔g8
14	f3	

This enables the white king to advance.

14	...	♖a1
15	a5	♔f8
16	a6	♔g8
17	♔g3	♖a4

Black can only wait, and must keep his rook ready to stop the white a-pawn.

| 18 | f4 | f5 |

This attempts to stop the white king.

19	h5	♔h8
20	h6	♔g8
21	♖g7+	♔h8
22	a7	

White is now threatening the decisive ♖b7, ♖b8+ and a8♕ winning. It appears that Black can draw because his king is stalemated so he can sacrifice his rook, but this is not the case.

| 22 | ... | ♖a3+ |

| 23 | ♔h4 | ♖h3+ |

Of course, if White takes the rook Black is stalemated and the game is a draw.

24	♔g5	♖h5+
25	♔f6	♖xh6+
26	♖g6	

Black resigned because now if 27 ... ♖xg6+ 28 ♔xg6 ♔g8 29 a8♕ mate.

We have seen that weak pawns can often lose the game, so take care to avoid them where possible.

7   MORE ENDINGS

In chapter 2 we examined two basic endgame skills: checkmating a lone king and promoting a pawn, both *essential* skills which should become easy with constant use. In this chapter endings with extra pieces are considered.

Why is it so important to learn these endgame techniques? Because in the opening and middlegame it is often possible to make a mistake and recover from it, whereas in the endgame it is hardly ever possible to recover from a mistake.

Study of the endgame is very important if you want to become a strong player, for it is no good building up a winning position in the opening and middlegame if you cannot finish the game properly.

In chapter 2 we looked at situations where one side had a passed pawn (i.e. not obstructed) and was pushing it through to promotion. Now let us consider examples where both sides have passed pawns which cannot be prevented from queening.

QUEEN VERSUS ADVANCED PASSED PAWN

In this position if it were Black's move then the game would end in a draw as follows:

1	...	d2
2	h8♕	d1♕

Both sides have a queen, but neither side can make progress.

If it White's move then White can win by

1	h8♕	d2

Here Black's pawn has reached the seventh rank and in the first part of this chapter we will consider the struggle between queen and pawn on the seventh rank.

This is a basic position to know. Black has a centre pawn on the seventh. A centre pawn is either a d- or e-pawn. In this position with White to move White always win however far away his king, apart from exceptional cases where the white king blocks the action of his own queen.

The winning method is as follows. White forces the black king to block the pawn and then bring his own king up.

1	♕b2	

Pinning the pawn.

1	...	♚e1
2	♕b4	♚e2
3	♕e4+	♚f2
4	♕d3	♚e1
5	♕e3+	♚d1

White has achieved his aim and now brings his king up.

6	♔b7	♚c2
7	♕e2	♚c1
8	♕c4+	♚b2
9	♕d3	♚c1
10	♕c3+	♚d1

11	♔c6	♚e2
12	♕c2	♚e1
13	♕e4+	♚f2
14	♕d3	♚e1
15	♕e3+	♚d1
16	♔c5	♚c2
17	♕e2	♚c1
18	♕c4+	♚b2
19	♕d3	♚c1
20	♕c3+	♚d1
21	♔d4	♚e2
22	♕c2	♚e1
23	♕e4+	♚f1
24	♕d3+	♚e1
25	♕e3+	♚d1
26	♔c3	♚c1
27	♕xd2+	♚b1
28	♕b2 mate.	

The same method works with a knight's pawn (b- or g-pawn). When the pawn is on the bishop's or rook's file the winning chances are considerably diminished because of stalemate possibilities. First let us consider the pawn on the rook's file.

Suppose White tries to implement the same plan:

1	♕g2+	♚b1
2	♕f1+	♚b2
3	♕b5+	♚c2
4	♕a4+	♚b2

5	♕b4+	♚c2
6	♕a3	♚b1
7	♕b3+	♚a1

The vital difference now is that White cannot move his king since Black will then be stalemated. White can make no progress and the game is drawn.

Now let us consider the pawn on the bishop's file (c- or f-files).

1	♕b2	♚d1
2	♕d4+	♚e2
3	♕c3	♚d1
4	♕d3+	♚c1

White forces the black king to block the pawn and then brings his king.

5	♚b7	♚b2
6	♕d2	♚b1
7	♕b4+	♚a2
8	♕c3	♚b1
9	♕b3+	♚a1!

This is the point! Black is not compelled to block the pawn by 9 ... ♚c1, since White cannot capture the pawn now: 10 ♕xc2 is stalemate. White can make no further progress and the game is drawn.

Sometimes it is possible to win against a rook's pawn or a bishop's pawn when the king is near enough. The danger of stalemate can be averted by allowing the pawn to queen and using the time to create a mating position.

The white king is close, enabling White to win as follows:

1	♕g2+	♚b1
2	♚c4	a1♕
3	♚b3	

Despite his queen, Black cannot prevent mate. Again, with a bishop's pawn, it is possible to win if the king is close enough.

1	♕g2	♚b1

2	♔b3	c1♛
3	♛a2 mate.	

This concludes our study of the queen against the advanced passed pawn. This ending often occurs in practice, and a close study of it win will pay dividends.

QUEEN VERSUS ROOK

This is quite a common ending. The queen normally wins against a rook, apart from a few special cases, but the win is usually difficult. The key to this ending is the tremendous power of the queen; if the rook gets separated from its own king, then the queen can often capture it by a series of checks ending in a fork. The win is brought about by forcing back the enemy king until it has no moves. The rook must then be moved away and it can be won by the queen.

Here we have the enemy king and rook huddled together in the middle of the board and the first stage is to force them back.

1	♛f3+	♚e5
2	♛e4+	♚d6
3	♔d4	

White must use both his king and queen to drive back the enemy king.

3	...	♜c6
4	♛e5+	♚d7
5	♔d5	♜c7
6	♛e6+	♚d8

It is important now for White not to fall into a stalemate trap. 7 ♔d6? would be a bad mistake because of 7 ... ♖c6+ 8 ♔xc6 and Black is stalemated.

7	♕g8+	♔e7
8	♕g7+	♔d8
9	♕f8+	♔d7

10	**♕f4**

By attacking the rook White forces the black king to retreat or the rook to move away, e.g. 1 ... ♖c3 2 ♕f5+ and no matter where the black king moves White wins the rook with a check on his next move.

10	...	♔c8

10 ... ♖b7 11 ♕f7+ ♔c8 12 ♕e8+ ♔c7 13 ♔c5 wins.

11	♔d6	♔b8

11 ... ♖d7+ 12 ♔c6 wins.

12	♕e5	♖b7

113

13	♔c6+	♚a8
14	♕a1+	♚b8
15	♕a5	

One of the basic winning positions. The black rook must move away from the king. Here are the black alternatives:

15	...	♚c8
16	♕a6 wins.	
15	...	♖b3
16	♕d8+	♚a7
17	♕d4+	♚b8
18	♕f4+	♚a7
19	♕a4+ wins the rook.	
15	...	♖b1
16	♕d8+	♚a7
17	♕d4+	♚a8
18	♕h8+	♚a7
19	♕h7+ wins the rook.	
15	...	♖e7
16	♕d8+ wins the rook.	
15	...	♖f7
16	♕e5+	♚a7
17	♕e3+	♚b8
18	♕e8+ wins the rook.	
15	...	♖h7
16	♕e5+	♚a8
17	♕a1+	♚b8
18	♕b1+ wins the rook.	

114

The queen does not always win; sometimes the player with the rook can force a stalemate position.

If it is Black's move in this position he can force a draw as follows.

1	...	♖h7+
2	♔g2	♖g7+
3	♔f3	♖f7+
4	♔g4	

4 ♔e4 ♖e7 draws.

4	...	♖g7+
5	♔f5	♖f7+
6	♔g6	♖g7+
7	♔h6	

7 ♔f6 ♖g6+! 8 ♔xg6 stalemate.

7	...	♖h7+!

8 ♔xh7 is stalemate, so White cannot win.

MORE KING AND PAWN ENDINGS

We have seen in chapter 2 that where one side has a passed pawn, the defending side must attempt to stop the pawn with his king. Therefore the threat of promoting a pawn will force the defending side to a particular part of the board leaving other sectors undefended.

In our first example White already has a passed a-pawn and the black king must rush to the queenside to stop this pawn from queening. The white king can then move to the kingside and gobble up the black pawns.

Fischer-Larsen
Denver 1971

The game continued:

| 1 | &d4 | &d6 |
| 2 | a5 | f6 |

If Black moves his king towards the white pawn – 2 ... &c6, then the white king invades – 3 &e5.

3	a6	&c6
4	a7	&b7
5	&d5	

The white king is ready to eat the black pawns, so Black tries to trick White.

| 5 | ... | h4 |

Black tempts White to take this pawn, when the game would be drawn as follows: 6 gxh4 &xa7 7 &e6 f5 8 &e5 &b7 9 h5 gxh5

116

10 ♔xf5 ♚c7 11 ♔g5 ♚d7 12 ♔xh5 ♚e7 and Black reaches f8 with a draw because of the rook's pawn.

6   ♔e6

Black resigned.

A likely continuation would have been: 6 ... f5 7 ♔f6 hxg3 8 hxg3 ♚xa7 9 ♔xg6 ♚b7 10 ♔xf5 ♚c7 11 ♔f6 ♚d7 12 g4 ♚e8 ♔g7 ♚e7 14 g5 ♚e8 15 g6 ♚e7 16 ♔h7 and White queens his pawn.

Here White already had a distant passed pawn on the queenside but the same play can occur when a player has a pawn majority on one side.

It is Black to move. White has a pawn majority of 2-1 on the queenside and is threatening to create a passed pawn with b5. So Black must play:

1	...	♚e6
2	♔e3	♚e5
3	b5	axb5
4	axb5	♚d5
5	♔f4	♚c5

5 ... h6 6 b6 ♚c6 7 ♔e5 and White wins the pawns by ♔f6 next move.

6	♔g5	♚xb5
7	♔h6	♚c4
8	♔xh7	g5
9	♔g6	g4
10	♔xf5	

White wins the remaining black pawn and the game.

In the two preceding examples, the black pawn majority was ineffective, but in the next one the situation is different.

Here Black has a 2-1 pawn majority on the queenside and White has a 3-2 majority on the kingside. Black wins as follows:

1	...	h5
2	f5+	gxf5
3	gxf5+	♔f6
4	♔f4	

Here White's passed pawn is not so effective as it is in the middle of the board. Black's pawns are well placed on the side of the board.

4	...	b6
5	♔e4	a6

Black is preparing to create a passed pawn with ... b5.

6	♔d5	♔xf5
7	♔c6	b5

Black exchanges off the pawns on the queenside leaving his own king free to capture the white h-pawn.

8	axb5	axb5
9	♔xb5	♔g4
10	♔c4	♔xh4
11	♔d3	♔g3
12	♔e2	♔g2

Black cuts the white king off from reaching f1 and thus queens his h-pawn which now cannot be stopped. It is worth watching out for pawn sacrifices to create a winning passed pawn.

Here White can create a winning passed pawn as follows:

1	b5	cxb5
2	a5	bxa5
3	c5	a4
4	c6	a3
5	c7	a2
6	c8♕+	

and White wins by bringing his queen back to capture the a-pawn.

Black may play:

1	...	axb5
2	c5	bxc5
3	a5	c4
4	a6	c3
5	a7	c2
6	a8♕+	

winning for White.

Pomar-Cuadras
Olot 1974

119

Black broke through to queen as follows:

| | **1** | ... | **f4** |

If 2 exf4 h4 3 gxh4 g3 4 fxg3 e3 and the black pawn queens.

| | **2** | **♔d5** | **h4!** |

Black is threatening to queen a pawn with ... h3.

| | **3** | **♔xe4** |

If 3 gxf4 h3 wins; or 3 gxh4 g3 4 fxg3 fxe3 wins.

| | **3** | ... | **f3!** |

Not 3 ... h3 4 gxh3 gxh3 5 ♔f3 stopping the pawn.

| | **4** | **gxf3** | **h3** |

White resigns since he cannot stop the black pawn from queening and winning the game.

MINOR PIECES: THE BISHOP AND THE KNIGHT

The minor pieces were both given an approximate value of 3 in the opening chapter, but often one is much stronger than the other. If the position is open, there are plenty of open diagonals for the bishop to travel along, and the pawns are free to advance, then the bishop is a much better piece. The bishop is a long-range piece. A knight on the edge of the board can be trapped by a bishop.

Here the black knight cannot move without being captured by the white bishop, an example of a bishop dominating a knight in an endgame.

In the following position material is equal, but Black proved the advantage of a bishop versus knight on an open board.

Suttles-Tal
Hastings 1974

| 1 | ... | ♗e7! |

Black prepares to deploy his bishop on the fine square d6, where it will attack both the white b- and g-pawns.

| 2 | b5 | ♗d6 |

Now if White defends the pawn with 3 ♔f2 Black invades with 3 ... ♔c4 and gobbles up the white queenside pawns.

3	a5	♗xg3
4	♘b4+	♔c5
5	♘c6	

A clever try by White. He hopes for 5 ... ♔xb5 6 ♘xa7+ ♔xa5 7 ♘c6+ followed by capturing the black d-pawn and achieving a draw.

| 5 | ... | a6 |

White cannot capture the pawn without losing his knight.

| 6 | ♔d3 | |

White hopes now to capture the black d-pawn.

6	...	♗f2!
7	♘a7	axb5
8	a6	

Another trick. If Black plays 8 ... ♔b6, after 9 ♘xb5 he cannot capture the white knight because of 10 a7.

8	...	b4
9	♘b5	♔b6
10	a7	♔b7
11	♘d6+	♔xa7
12	♘xf5	b3

	13	♘d6	♚b6

White resigned.

White cannot defend any more. If 14 ♘c4+ ♚b5 15 ♘d2 ♚b4 and the black king will penetrate the white position.

When the position is blocked and the pawns are fixed, the knight is a better piece. Sometimes the bishop is hampered by its own pawns and sometimes by the enemy pawns. When it is hampered by its own pawns it is called a 'bad' bishop.

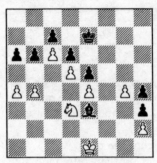

Garcia-Quinteros
Moscow Interzonal 1982

Here the white knight is a much better piece than the black bishop. Several of Black's pawns are fixed on the dark squares, which hampers the bishop. White concluded the game as follows:

	1	b5	a5

If Black exchanges on b5, the white knight can leap to a6 via b4.

	2	♚e2	♗g1
	3	♚f1	♗xh2
	4	g5!!	

The key to White's pawn sacrifice. If the black king attempts to stop the white g-pawn with 4 ... ♚f7 White wins by 5 ♘c5. Now if Black captures the knight by 5 ... bxc5 then 6 b6 cxb6 7 c7 and queens, or if 5 ... dxc5 6 d6 cxd6 7 c7 and queens. If instead after 5 ♘c5 Black plays 5 ... ♚g6, White will win by 6 ♘e6 and 7 ♘xc7.

	4	...	♗f4
	5	♘xf4	exf4
	6	g6	f3
	7	♚g1	

White must prevent 7 ... h2. On g1 the white king can hold both black pawns.

7	...	♔f6
8	e5+!	dxe5
9	d6	e4
10	d7	

and Black resigned because of 10 ... ♔e7 11 g7.

MINOR PIECES VERSUS PAWNS

When a player is a piece up in the endgame, he will normally win, but there are positions where an extra minor piece is not sufficient to win, and sometimes loses. This happens when the player who is a piece down has more pawns; especially dangerous are positions where there is the possibility of creating a distant passed pawn on each wing.

Black has a bishop for two pawns, but here the bishop proves unable to stop the white infantry.

1	h6	gxh6
2	g6!	

Not 2 gxh6 ♔b8 3 ♔e5 ♗a5 4 ♔d4 ♗d8 with a draw.

2	...	♗f6+
3	♔d5	♔b8
4	♔e6	♗c3
5	♔d7	♗e5
6	g7	♗xg7
7	c7+	

and White queens a pawn.

123

ROOK VERSUS PAWNS

The rook can often deal with passed pawns but cannot cope with two united passed pawns on the sixth rank.

Black wins by

1	...	g2
2	♖g4	h2
3	♖xg2	h1♕

with a winning advantage of queen versus rook. Even if it is White to move, he still cannot stop the pawns.

1	♖g4	h2
2	♖h4	g2

and Black wins.

ROOK AND PAWN ENDINGS

One of the commonest endings is when one side has a rook and a pawn and the other side just a rook. Then the struggle revolves around whether the pawn can be promoted. The defending side *should* be able to draw if he can get his king in front of the pawn, but if he cannot do this, and the pawn is cut off from the defending king, then the attacking side can often win.

A key position to learn is the Lucena position.

The black king is cut off, but the white king cannot yet get out from in front of the pawn. White wins as follows:

The Lucena position

	1	Rf4!	Rh1

1 ... Ke7 2 Re4+ Kf6 3 Kf8 wins.

	2	Re4+	Kd7
	3	Kf7	Rf1+
	4	Kg6	Rg1+
	5	Kf6	Rf1+
	6	Kg5	Rg1+
	7	Rg4	

The white king has been sheltered from the checks and Black cannot stop the pawn from queening.

So in order to win with a rook and pawn against rook, the defending king must be cut off from the pawn, and in order to advance the pawn, it must be supported by the king.

ROOK ENDGAMES

When one side has a passed pawn, the best position for the friendly rook is behind the passed pawn. This is because as the pawn advances the rook becomes more powerful.

Here White's rook is stuck in front of the pawn and cannot move without it being lost. The white king can come over to the pawn, but has no shelter from checks by the enemy rook. So this position is a draw. Black must be careful over the positioning of his king, since White can win if the king is not on g7 or h7.

Here White wins by 1 ♖h8 ♖xa7 2 ♖h7+ skewering the black rook.

If the king is on the third rank White wins by 1 ♖g8+ ♔h7 2 a8♕.

ROOK AND PAWN VERSUS ROOK AND PAWN

Endings with one pawn each normally result in a draw, but sometimes one side has a big enough advantage to win.

Alekhine-Bogoljubow
Match 1929

In this position material is equal, but White's passed pawn is close to queening. Black will have to give up his rook for the white pawn and then it will depend on whether the white king and rook can stop the black pawn. Play continued:

	1	...	♔g4?

This is the losing mistake. Black should play 1 ... ♔e4 in order to impede the march of the white king back to stop the pawn. Black draws after 1 ... ♔e4 2 b7 f5 3 b8♕ ♖xb8 4 ♖xb8 f4 5 ♖b4+ ♔e3 6 ♔d5 f3 7 ♖b3+ ♔e2 8 ♔e4 f2 9 ♖b2+ ♔e1 10 ♔e3 f1♘ with a drawn position of rook against knight.

	2	b7	f5
	3	b8♕	♖xb8
	4	♖xb8	f4
	5	♔d5	f3
	6	♔e4	f2
	7	♖f8	♔g3
	8	♔e3	

Black resigned because he cannot queen the pawn and White captures it next move.

In more complicated rook endings the same general ideas apply; the struggle also revolves around the creation of a passed pawn and then its promotion.

OTHER ENDINGS

Opposite bishop endings, in which both sides have a bishop but of opposite colours and where the material is equal in other respects, often end in a draw. This is because the pawns can avoid attack if they occupy squares of the opposite colour to the enemy bishop. Even when one side has a material advantage, the game is still often a draw.

Here White has two extra pawns but he cannot win:

1	♔e6	♗b4
2	♗e4	♔d8
3	♔f7	♗a3
4	e6	♗b4
5	c7+	♔xc7
6	e7	♗xe7

with a draw.

With bishops of the same colour there are more winning chances.

Here White wins easily:

1	♔g5	♔d8
2	♔f6	♗b3
3	e6	♗a2
4	e7+	♔e8

5   ♗g6+ and wins

Knight and pawn endings are difficult to handle and, as in other endings, it is important to use the king actively.

Barcza-Simagin 1949

Here White has an extra pawn, but Black's pawn supported by both pieces is the decisive factor.

| 1 | ... | d3 |
| 2 | ♔f1 | ♘c3 |

Black threatens to play 3 ... d2, queening the pawn.

3	♔e1	♔d4
4	♔d2	♘e4+
5	♔c1	

White hopes for 5 ... ♔e3 6 ♘b5 d2+ 7 ♔c2 ♔e2 8 ♘d4+ ♔e1 9 ♘f3+ with a draw, but Black has a subtle move which prevents the white knight from coming back to defend.

| 5 | ... | ♘d6 |
| 6 | ♔d2 | |

6 ♘c6+ ♔c3 7 ♘e7 d2+ 8 ♔d1 ♘e4 9 ♘d5+ ♔c4 10 ♘b6+ ♔d3 and Black mates next move.

6	...	♘c4+
7	♔c1	d2+
8	♔c2	♔e3
9	♘b5	

This position is similar to that in the note to move 5, for if 9 ... ♔e2 10 ♘d4+ draws, but now Black plays a typical knight sacrifice to push the pawn home.

| 9 | ... | ♘a3+ |

White resigned because after 10 ♘xa3 ♔e2 the pawn queens.

8 MORE OPENINGS

We have already seen some of the basic symmetrical openings where Black replies to 1 e4 with 1 ... e5 and to 1 d4 with 1 ... d5. There are many other openings, both symmetrical and asymmetrical. We shall first consider examples of asymmetrical openings, and then, later in the section, look at some more difficult examples of symmetrical openings.

THE FRENCH DEFENCE

	1	e4	e6

Here Black prepares to attack the white e-pawn by ... d5. White will often advance in the centre with e5 in response to ... d5, and the centre will be blocked. White will have a pawn on d4 to support the pawn on e5, and Black will try to undermine this pawn centre with ... c5.

	2	d4	d5
	3	♘d2	

This is called the Tarrasch Variation of the French Defence. White defends his pawn on e4 with a knight. The alternatives are 3 ♘c3 ♗b4 and 3 e5, the Advance Variation.

130

3   ...   ♞f6

Black again puts pressure on the white pawn on e4.

4   e5

White advances and now we have the pawn structure typical of the French Defence.

4   ...   ♞fd7
5   c3   c5

Black is attacking the pawn on d4 which supports the advanced white pawn on e5.

6   ♗d3   ♞c6
7   ♞e2   ♛b6
8   ♞f3

Black is attacking the white pawn on d4 three times and White has defended the pawn three times. If White can retain his pawn centre he will have an advantage because he has more space and the black pieces are cramped. So Black eliminates the white pawn centre by attacking it head on.

8   ...   cxd4
9   cxd4   f6

Black attacks the head of the pawn chain.

10   exf6   ♞xf6
11   0-0   ♗d6

Black has now freed his game but has a weak pawn on e6.

12   ♞c3   0-0
13   ♗e3   ♛d8

Black hopes to deploy the queen on the kingside for a possible attack on the white king.

131

14   ♗g5

The game is equal. Black has a weak pawn on e6 and his queen's bishop has little scope, which is typical of the French Defence. Black has possibilities of a kingside attack, however, which he should commence with 14 ... ♕e8 with the idea of ... ♕h5.

THE CARO-KANN DEFENCE

	1	e4	c6

This is similar to the French Defence in that Black prepares the advance ... d5, attacking the white pawn on e4.

	2	d4	d5
	3	♘c3	

The alternatives are 3 e5 ♗f5 and 3 exd5 cxd5 with, in both cases, a satisfactory game for Black.

	3	...	dxe4
	4	♘xe4	♘d7
	5	♘f3	♘gf6
	6	♘xf6+	♘xf6
	7	♘e5	

White prevents the pin of his knight by ... ♗g4 and prepares the attacking 8 ♗c4.

	7	...	♗e6
	8	♗e2	g6
	9	0-0	♗g7
	10	c4	0-0

11 &e3

White has a slight advantage because of his well placed knight on e5. Black has a sound game and can play to exchange off the white knight with ... &d7.

ALEKHINE'S DEFENCE

1 e4 &f6

This is a provocative defence tempting White to attack the knight with e5. Black hopes to undermine White's advanced pawn centre.

2	e5	&d5
3	d4	d6
4	&f3	&g4

Black pins the white knight and hopes to attack the white pawns on d4 and e5.

133

5	♗e2	e6
6	0-0	♗e7
7	c4	♘b6

White has gained some time by attacking the black knight, but Black has counterplay against the white pawns.

8	♘c3	0-0
9	♗e3	d5
10	c5	♗xf3
11	gxf3	

White captures with the pawn in order to avoid the black knight coming in to c4 – 11 ♗xf3 ♘c4.

11	...	♘c8

Now 11 ... ♘c4 12 ♗xc4 dxc4 13 ♕a4 wins a pawn.

The game is unbalanced with both sides having equal chances. White has a big pawn centre and the two bishops, but Black has the sounder pawn structure and counter-attacking chances.

134

THE MODERN DEFENCE

	1	e4	g6

This is similar to Alekhine's Defence in character. Black offers White the opportunity to create a pawn centre and then prepares to undermine it.

	2	d4	d6
	3	♘c3	♘f6
	4	♘f3	

This is one of White's quietest set-ups against the Modern Defence. White can also try the aggressive 4 f4.

	4	...	♗g7
	5	♗e2	0-0
	6	0-0	♗g4

Black prepares to create play on the central dark squares by 7 ... ♘c6 and 8 ... e5.

135

7 &e3 &c6

8 ♕d2

White prepares to bring his queen's rook into play on d1.

8 ... e5

9 d5 &e7

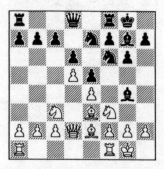

White's space advantage gives him a slight edge.

THE SICILIAN DEFENCE

1 e4 c5

This is one of the most popular replies to 1 e4. It is a counter-attack rather than a defence. Black normally aims for queen-side play whereas White concentrates on the kingside. Black often has considerable counterplay down the c-file.

2 &f3

White has the alternatives 2 &c3 or 2 f4, choosing not to open the centre with d4. On the other hand, 2 &f3 prepares to play 3 d4.

2 ... d6

Black has a wide range of moves here; he can play 2 ... e6, 2 ...

136

♘c6, 2 ... a6, 2 ... g6 and others.

	3	d4	cxd4
	4	♘xd4	♘f6
	5	♘c3	

Now Black has a choice: 5 ... g6 (the Dragon Variation); 5 ... e6 (the Scheveningen Variation); 5 ... ♘c6; and the line given below.

	5	...	a6

This is the Najdorf Variation. Black prepares to expand on the queenside with ... b5.

	6	♗g5	

White threatens to double Black's pawns with ♗xf6.

	6	...	e6
	7	f4	♗e7
	8	♕f3	♕c7
	9	0-0-0	

A typical Sicilian position. White is preparing to launch a kingside pawn storm, whilst Black has counter-attacking prospects on the queenside.

137

Queenside Openings

We have seen some openings where Black answers 1 d4 with 1 ... d5. However, there are a number of openings where Black prefers not to occupy the centre with pawns, but to control it with pieces.

THE NIMZO-INDIAN DEFENCE

1	d4	♘f6
2	c4	e6
3	♘c3	♗b4

White was threatening to obtain control of the centre with e4, but Black pins the white knight and prevents it (4 e4 ♘xe4). White has a number of different alternatives here, and we shall look at three of them:

A

4	a3	

White immediately forces Black to give up a bishop for a knight. White's plan is to form a large pawn centre and then use his two bishops to attack the black king. The black plan is to fix the white centre, keep the white bishops stifled and eventually attack White's doubled pawns.

4	...	♗xc3+
5	bxc3	c5
6	e3	b6
7	♗d3	♗b7
8	f3	♘c6
9	♘e2	0-0

	10	e4	♞e8

Black retreats his knight. He wishes to avoid White pinning this knight by ♗g5. In addition, this allows Black to reply to the advance f4 with ... f5.

	11	♗e3	d6
	12	0-0	♞a5

Black prepares to attack the weak white c-pawn by ... ♗a6.

	13	♞g3	♛d7
	14	f4	f5

Black has a good position. He can secure his kingside against a white attack by ... g6 and ... ♞g7. Later he can play to win the white c-pawn by ... ♗a6 and ... ♖c8.

B

	4	♛c2	c5

Black attacks the white centre.

	5	dxc5	0-0

139

	6	♘f3	♘a6
	7	♗d2	♘xc5
	8	a3	♗xc3
	9	♘xc3	♘ce4

Black attacks the white bishop on c3. White cannot retain the advantage of the two bishops easily since after 10 ♗d4 b6 followed by ... ♗b7 and ... ♖c8 Black has a fine game.

	10	e3	b6
	11	♗e2	♗g7
	12	0-0	♖c8
	13	♗b4	♖e8

Black has good play on the semi-open c-file.

C

	4	e3

This is White's strongest line against the Nimzo-Indian.

	4	...	0-0
	5	♘f3	d5
	6	♗d3	c5

Black attacks the white centre.

	7	0-0	dxc4
	8	♗xc4	cxd4
	9	exd4	b6
	10	♗g5	♗b7
	11	♕e2	♗xc3
	12	bxc3	♘bd7

The position is equal. White has the two bishops and attacking chances against the black king. Black has counterplay down the c-file.

THE QUEEN'S INDIAN DEFENCE

	1	d4	♘f6
	2	c4	e6
	3	♘f3	

White avoids the Nimzo-Indian Defence. Here Black could transpose to a Queen's Gambit with ... d5.

	3	...	b6

Black plays to control the central light squares.

	4	g3	♗b7
	5	♗g2	♗e7
	6	♘c3	♘e4

Black plays to exchange off knights and also paves the way to play ... f5, controlling e4.

	7	♗d2	f5
	8	d5	♗f6

9	♕c2	♘a6
10	0-0	

White has a slight advantage.

THE KING'S INDIAN DEFENCE

1	d4	♘f6
2	c4	g6

This is a fighting defence to 1 d4 where Black hopes to gain play on the central dark squares and make use of his fianchettoed king's bishop.

3	♘c3	♗g7
4	e4	d6
5	f3	

White solidifies his pawn centre and also prepares 6 ♗e3.

5	...	0-0
6	♗e3	e5

Black stakes a claim in the centre.

7	d5	♘h5

A typical manoeuvre in the King's Indian. Black prepares the freeing advance ... f5.

	8	♕d2

White prepares to castle queenside.

8	...	f5
9	0-0-0	♞d7
10	exf5	gxf5
11	♗d3	

White has a slight advantage.

THE GRUNFELD DEFENCE

This is similar to the King's Indian Defence except that Black plays ... c5 rather than ... e5.

1	d4	♞f6
2	c4	g6
3	♞c3	d5

The starting position of the Grünfeld Defence. Again, Black allows White to build up a big pawn centre in the hope that he will be able to attack it later.

4	cxd5	♞xd5
5	e4	♞xc3
6	bxc3	c5
7	♗e3	♗g7
8	♗c4	♞c6

Black is attacking the pawn on d4 and White is defending it.

9	♘e2	cxd4
10	cxd4	0-0
11	0-0	♗g4
12	f3	♘a5
13	♗d3	♗e6

The game is equal. White has a strong pawn centre but Black has a pawn majority on the queenside and good chances if an endgame is reached.

THE ENGLISH OPENING

1   c4

This opening has become a popular choice for White in recent years.

1	...	e5
2	♘c3	♘f6
3	g3	♗b4
4	♗g2	0-0
5	♘f3	♖e8

Black has developed his pieces simply and sensibly. White has potential pressure down the long diagonal, but Black has play in the centre.

6	0-0	e4
7	♘e1	♗xc3
8	dxc3	h6

Black prevents an annoying pin with ♗g5.

9	♘c2	d6
10	♘e3	♘bd7

The chances are equal. White has the two bishops but Black has the better pawn structure and a strong advanced pawn on e4.

145

Further Symmetrical Openings with 1 e4 e5

THE PETROFF DEFENCE

1	e4	e5
2	♘f3	♘f6

A solid defence and a good one. Black counter-attacks the white e-pawn instead of defending his own.

3	♘xe5	d6

3 ... ♘xe4 4 ♕e2 ♕e7 5 ♕xe4 d6 6 d4 is much better for White.

4	♘f3	♘xe4
5	d4	

5 ♕e2 ♕e7 does not lead to any advantage for White.

5	...	d5
6	♗d3	♗e7
7	0-0	♘c6

8   ♖e1   ♝g4

Now White cannot win a pawn with 9 ♗xe4 dxe4 10 ♖xe4 because of 10 ... ♗xf3 11 ♕xf3 ♘xd4.

9   c3   f5
10   ♘bd2   0-0
11   ♕b3   ♚h8

This sharp position offers equal chances to both sides.

THE OPEN DEFENCE TO THE RUY LOPEZ

In the first chapter on openings we saw the Closed Defence to the Ruy Lopez. The Open Defence leads to a completely different type of game.

1   e4   e5
2   ♘f3   ♘c6
3   ♗b5   a6
4   ♗a4   ♘f6
5   0-0   ♘xe4

5 ... ♝e7 is the Closed Defence.

	6	d4	b5
	7	♝b3	d5

Black supports his advanced knight. 7 ... exd4 8 ♖e1 d5 9 ♝xd5 ♛xd5 10 ♞c3 is difficult for Black.

| | 8 | dxe5 | ♝e6 |

Chances are balanced. Black has chances on the queenside with his majority; White has chances on the kingside.

Further Symmetrical Openings with 1 d4 d5

THE TARRASCH DEFENCE

	1	d4	d5
	2	c4	e6
	3	♞c3	c5

Black strives for active play at the cost of an isolated pawn.

	4	cxd5	exd5
	5	♞f3	♞c6
	6	g3	

White fianchettoes his bishop in order to bear down on Black's pawn on d5.

	6	...	♞f6
	7	♝g2	♝e7
	8	0-0	0-0
	9	♝g5	

9	...	cxd4
10	♘xd4	

White has slightly the better chances because of the isolated black pawn on d5.

9 GENERAL ADVICE

This chapter is devoted to some practical aspects of playing chess and how to improve. I have included a note on chess-playing computers, as these are becoming an increasingly popular feature of the amateur game.

THE OPENINGS

There are a few general principles which can be applied to the openings. We saw in the introductory chapter that pieces are at their most powerful in the centre of the board, and from this a number of opening principles can be derived:

(1) Develop your pieces quickly to control central squares.

(2) Do not make too many pawn moves in the opening because the enemy will gain control of the centre with his pieces.

(3) Develop the minor pieces (knights and bishops) first. It is normal to develop the knights before the bishops because the knight is weak at the edge of the board and exerts much more influence in the centre.

(4) Do not bring the queen out too early; the queen is a very valuable piece and if attacked by enemy minor pieces will normally have to retreat.

(5) Castle early; this brings the king into safety and also helps the development of the rooks.

(6) Try not to move the same piece too many times in the opening; instead try to develop each piece by moving it once only.

THE MIDDLEGAME

The middlegame is more complex and therefore general principles do not enter into consideration so much, but here are a few helpful ideas to bear in mind:

(1) It is useful to have a plan of campaign. Whether you choose to launch an attack against the enemy king, or a breakthrough in the centre or whatever, a plan is useful as

indecisive play can often lead to disaster.

(2)   A general rule which is most applicable in the middlegame, though also for other stages of the game, is to examine your opponent's last move to find out:

(a) Whether it contains a threat against which you must guard.

(b) If you can attack or capture any of your opponent's pieces.

(c) If your planned reply leaves your own pieces susceptible to attack.

(3)   If you cannot decide what to do, examine your pieces to see if the position of any of them can be improved.

(4)   Try to exchange badly placed pieces, or exchange your opponent's well placed pieces; the corollary is to avoid the exchange of your well placed pieces.

THE ENDGAME

In the endgame the following principles are worth remembering:

(1)   Use the king actively; usually there is no danger of the king being checkmated and it can become a strong fighting piece.

(2)   Try to place the rooks on open files.

(3)   Try to use your rooks to attack the enemy pawns.

(4)   Exchange off pawns in order to create a passed pawn, to tie down the enemy pieces.

HOW TO IMPROVE

You may have played a few games and are wondering how you can improve your chess. Your general approach to the game is very important – you should treat all games seriously. Do not take back moves in friendly games; this is not allowed in a serious game and is thus a bad habit.

One of the best ways of improving is to record games for future reference and study; they can be written in a chess score book (available from a chess equipment supplier). After every game you can replay the game and try to find any mistakes; it is extremely unlikely that there will not be any mistakes on your part, even if you have won. You can often discuss the game afterwards with your opponent – this is known as a 'post mortem'. If the game is recorded in a score book, then you can look up the opening in an openings book, and the endgame in an endgame book, to see how your play compares with that of experts. This study of the game after you play is most important and can prove invaluable if you reach the same positions again.

At first you may only play chess against friends or at school, but if you want to play against other serious players, you should go to a chess club. Most small towns have a chess club, and most cities have several. Your local library may have details of the nearest ones, but you can also get information by contacting the British Chess Federation at 9a Grand Parade, St Leonards on Sea, East Sussex (telephone: Hastings 442500).

Chess clubs vary in size and membership fees, so you may have to go to several clubs before you find a suitable one.

At a chess club you will find many people playing games using chess clocks (it is normal for all serious games of chess to be played with them). A chess clock consists of two clocks joined together. The players each push a button, when they have made their own move, to stop one clock and start the other, so that each clock records the thinking time of one player.

When trying to improve it is best to play opponents who are slightly stronger than you are and not to play repeatedly against the same person.

Chess books are numerous and are invaluable to improvement; a good starting point is a reference book on the openings, which lists them all and gives a few variations in each. An endgame reference book is also useful for the occasions when a game is adjourned (stopped at a certain time but to be played on later).

There are also a number of chess magazines which publish the latest ideas and news of tournaments; two of the best are:

Chess, Sutton Coldfield, Warwickshire;

British Chess Magazine, 9 Market Street, St Leonards on Sea, East Sussex.

CHESS COMPUTERS

As well as going to a chess club and competing in chess tournaments you can play at home with the aid of a chess computer. A chess computer only plays chess; there are chess programs available for most home computers but they are limited in scope.

Chess computers can be both instructive and provide endless enjoyment. The advantages of chess computers are that you can play against them at any time, they can play at different speeds and many will play at varying strengths. The chess computer can be used to solve problems and also to try out opening variations or any other positions that you wish to investigate. As there are many types of chess computer on the market, I think it is best to describe the basic features rather than individual models.

The first area to consider is how moves are communicated to and by the computer. There are many different types of move entry and reply, but some of the main ones are as follows:

1. Keying in
The move is entered by keying it in using algebraic notation. The move is normally shown on a display (liquid crystal). The computer should verify that the move is legal and then begin to work on its reply. The reply will be shown on the liquid crystal display.

2. Sensor boards
The move is transmitted to the computer by moving a piece on a board and pressing it down on the new square. The computer recognises the new square, verifies the move, then starts to work out its reply.

3. Cursor
On personal computers a cursor is used to indicate which piece should be moved and to which square.

All of these methods have advantages and disadvantages. For example, keying in requires a knowledge of algebraic notation (which you should know by now!).

The second major area to consider when purchasing a computer is rate and strength of play. In very simple terms, a computer chooses a move by pure calculation as, although concepts are known by the computer, it does not rely on these. Consequently, the longer the computer thinks about a move, the stronger the reply will be. A good computer could have the following levels of play:

a) an instantaneous reply level (weakest)
b) five seconds a move
c) ten seconds a move
d) general levels from fifteen seconds to three minutes a move
e) a level where the computer will think for up to 24 hours (strongest)

The 'infinite' (24 hour) level is very useful for playing chess by post or trying to analyse a particular position. It is also worth acquiring a computer which can play under normal competition time limits, which are 40 moves in two hours.

There are several other features which are worth mentioning. Some computers allow the user to see how they reach their decisions by displaying a number of alternative moves they are considering. Many of this type of computer also make an evaluation of the position, i.e. they will show who they think has the advantage. Some computers are modular, so that the program can be replaced by a stronger one when available. A printer attachment is useful if you wish to record your games; this is often easier on a home computer with a chess program than a chess computer.

Bibliography

Spike's Chess Primer, D.G.Ellison
Practical Chess Endings, P.Keres
Positional Chess, S.Taulbut
Chess Computer Handbook, D.Levy